CEO Pay and Shareholder Value

HELPING THE U.S.

WIN THE GLOBAL

ECONOMIC WAR

Ira T. Kay

Watson Wyatt Worldwide

T0301886

CRC Press
Taylor & Francis Group
Boca Raton London New York

CRC Press is an imprint of the
Taylor & Francis Group, an **informa** business

CRC Press
Taylor & Francis Group
6000 Broken Sound Parkway NW, Suite 300
Boca Raton, FL 33487-2742

© 1998 by Taylor & Francis Group, LLC
CRC Press is an imprint of Taylor & Francis Group, an Informa business

No claim to original U.S. Government works

ISBN 13: 978-1-57444-203-8 (hbk)

Visit the Taylor & Francis Web site at
http://www.taylorandfrancis.com

and the CRC Press Web site at
http://www.crcpress.com

Library of Congress Card Number 97-29274
Library of Congress Cataloging-in-Publication Data

Kay, Ira T.
    CEO pay and shareholder value : helping the U.S. win the global
economic war / by Ira T. Kay.
      p. cm.
    Includes index.
    ISBN 1-57444-203-1 (alk. paper)
    1. Chief executive officers- -Salaries, etc.- -United States.
2. Executive ability- -United States. 3. Stocks- -United States.
4. Stock ownership- -United States. 5. Competition, International.
I. Title.
HD4965.5.U6K388 1997
658.4′.0722—dc21
                                                 97-29274
                                                 CIP

Table of Contents

Acknowledgments

I would like to thank my colleagues at Watson Wyatt for their support while I was researching and writing this book. My clients have also served as a laboratory for testing many of the ideas presented.

Carter Prescott was invaluable to me as my editor and also as challenger of many of the ideas. She pushed me when I was slow and halted me when I moved too fast.

Bob McKee of Watson Wyatt's Marketing Department also was extremely helpful in making the manuscript come alive — both verbally and pictorially.

And finally, I would like to thank my wife, Carol, and my children Sarah, Ben and Jon, for their encouragement and support.

About the Author

Ira T. Kay is the Global Practice Director in charge of Watson Wyatt's Executive Compensation Practice. His primary objective is to help Watson Wyatt's clients to use compensation programs to create shareholder value. Mr. Kay has worked closely with U.S. public, international and private companies, helping them to develop annual and long-term incentive plans to drive their strategies.

Mr. Kay has held executive positions at the Hay Group, Kidder Peabody and Shearson Lehman Hutton.

Mr. Kay has a B.S. in Industrial and Labor Relations from Cornell University and a Ph.D. in Economics from Wayne State University. He has written and spoken broadly on strategic and executive compensation issues, and he has appeared on national radio and television. He is the author of *Value at the Top: Solutions to the Executive Compensation Crisis*, published by HarperCollins. He has presented analysis of critical executive compensation issues before the Securities and Exchange Commission (SEC), the Financial Accounting Standards Board (FASB) and a U.S. Senate subcommittee. He lives in New York City with his wife, Carol, and his three children.

Introduction

Establishing *stock price* as management's key performance measure
was one of the defining American capitalist reforms of the past
decade. It is a major source of global competitive advantage and
has helped create billions of dollars of value at thousands of U.S.
companies. Interestingly, stinging criticism of executive pay was
what prompted this move in the first place. Yet despite the fact
that tying performance to stock price appears to have substantially
benefited the U.S. economy overall — in addition to the executives
themselves — criticism of executive pay has not subsided.

U.S. executive pay has been under serious attack for nearly a
decade, although the nature of the attack has shifted dramatically
during that period. In the first phase, during the mid- to late 1980s,
critics argued that the compensation of executives, particularly CEOs,[1]
bore no relation to the financial or stock market performance of
their companies. The original critics included the media, government
and other agencies (SEC, IRS, FASB) and institutional shareholders
(particularly public employee pension funds).

While some of this criticism was overblown, it did trigger many
positive changes. Most importantly, by the early to mid-1990s,
there was a dramatic move to increase the relationship between
top executives' pay and the stock price of their company. This
occurred primarily through very large increases in stock option
grants and through an order-of-magnitude increase in executive
stock ownership. This new relationship has played a major — if
not dominant — role in motivating the massive increase in value of
the U.S. stock market.

---

1 Throughout this book, we primarily refer to CEO pay, but the perspective applies to
pay for all executive positions.

Stock market success, in turn, has caused the very high and rising levels of U.S. executive compensation that have prompted a second phase of criticism. This criticism takes many forms, but the most common are:

- CEOs are "not worth it;" CEO pay is too high in general;
- CEOs should not get rich by downsizing, in which downsized employees get lower paying jobs (part of the "income inequality" issue);
- CEO pay is still not related to performance;
- CEO pay went up because the stock market went up;
- The U.S. stock market would have performed just as well without stock options;
- Executive pay will not go down if the stock market goes down;
- CEO pay is too large a multiple of worker pay, and the gap is rising;
- CEO pay is part of a "winner-take-all" society;
- It will be disastrous if the United States "exports" its pay models; and
- The Japanese pay model is better.

The type of criticism has changed significantly in this second phase of the debate over executive pay. Current critics continue to include the media (with articles like the one in *The Economist*, entitled "Fat Cats and their Cream," or the 1997 headline in *Business Week*," Executive Pay: It's Out of Control") and those with political interests (from 1996 Republican Presidential candidate Pat Buchanan to President Clinton, who has commented on the "CEO multiple" being too high).

Most importantly, the *institutional shareholders* — the true owners of more than half of corporate America and the drivers of the stock ownership strategy — are *not* generally included in this current chorus. This is because they are the *beneficiaries* of this dramatic increase in value — with the size and security of *their* holders' pensions becoming much *greater*. As New York City Deputy Controller Jon Lukomnik, who oversees $55 billion in pension funds, told the *Financial Times*, "We don't care how much someone gets paid as long as we get paid; it's our dirty little secret."

The increase in executive stock ownership has had a major impact on the nature of corporate finance and structure over the same period. Indeed, the takeover craze of the mid- to late 1980s occurred precisely because CEOs did *not* maximize the value of their companies. Shareholders could get a better price when their assets were bought in LBOs and then spun off. This is in stark contrast with the current merger wave, where two or more *high*-value companies are combining to face jointly an uncertain economic future. And in many instances, their high value was created by strong stock-based compensation programs at each company.

It is all the more ironic, then, that many of the gains in CEO pay can be attributed to shareholder pressure to shift compensation to stock-based pay, as well as to government rules on executive pay. For example, the 1993 Clinton tax bill contains a provision [Section 162(m)] that puts a $1 million cap on deductible executive compensation — unless it is paid under a performance-based plan. New proxy rules from the SEC also force boards of directors to spell out specific goals that could unleash incentive pay. Another SEC mandate requires proxy statements to use graphs and tables, rather than simply prose, to make the connection between pay and performance easier to identify.

As a result, it is clear today that CEOs are much more the partners of shareowners, expected to take prudent risks and stay competitive to realize a higher market value for their companies. Despite the complaints of the media about high CEO pay, shareholder interests can be aligned with executives and the broad employee population. If solid strategies are chosen and if employees are highly productive, then shareholder investments increase, new plants are built, new technologies are introduced, new products are launched, new markets are entered, more and better jobs are created, stock prices rise, pensions are secured and pay increases — a great example of an upward spiral. Clearly the CEO is not alone, but acts in concert with other managers and all employees to create and implement these strategies. Proper executive compensation programs help to make this happen.

Moreover, because U.S. CEOs are motivated to focus on growth, globalization and efficiency, their pay is a competitive advantage in the global economy. Compare the U.S. experience with that of Japan, the industrialized country with executive pay practices completely the opposite of American ones. The American stock market has more than doubled in value during the 1990s, while the Japanese market has declined by 50 percent. There are many reasons aside from executive pay for the success of the U.S. economy and stock market over the past few years — ranging from low interest rates to reengineering. Nevertheless, we believe the role of compensation programs — especially those for executives — has been understated.

It is time for corporate boards to take the lead in stating the facts to the American public. They can start by explaining to shareholders and employees how business strategy, CEO pay and long-term financial security are all linked. In 1995 alone, the U.S. stock market created more than $1 trillion in value, several hundred billion of which went directly to pension funds. In comparison, the CEOs of all the *Fortune 500* companies took home *far* less than one percent of the stock market increase — or about $1 billion in pay. This is a small price to pay for economic security today and in retirement. In 1996, another $1 trillion in equity value was created. From 1994 to 1996, the total value of stock owned by American households rose from $5.7 trillion to $8.5 trillion, or nearly 50 percent.

It is frequently and skeptically asked whether CEO pay will go *down* if the stock market goes *down*. This is asked because one of the defenses of *high* pay is "the stock market caused it;" to make this a valid argument, of course, the converse must be true as well. We believe strongly that declining pay *will* happen and that it *should* happen. And given that the structure of pay contains so much stock, it seems impossible that it *could* not. Nevertheless, given our belief in the impact of these stock programs on executive motivation, we also believe strongly that any stock market decline would be *smaller* than if these programs did not exist.

The fundamental issue is not whether CEOs are overpaid. The critical question is, are they paid for their performance? And even more pertinent, does their compensation give them the right incentives to perform well for the one stakeholder group that takes most of the risks — the shareholders? The answer on both counts is yes.

CEO pay for performance has also increased employees' economic security by providing stronger job security for those who survive downsizing and for those who move on to new jobs with higher salaries, and by driving up the value of pension plans. Once again, U.S. pay practices are a source of international advantage. In Japan and Europe, fixed-pay programs, protectionism and guaranteed employment stifle competition and weaken their economies.

Many of the changes with which U.S. CEOs are familiar — such as increasing the number of independent outside directors, tying CEO pay to stock ownership and shareholder interests, and more complete disclosure of executive remuneration — are being transplanted to companies in other countries, such as Canada and the United Kingdom, which are not accustomed to such full disclosure and accountability. This is not to say that the U.S. model could be fully exported, if at all, to any other country. Each nation has its own unique culture and economy, which have a major influence on the efficacy of any compensation program. However, in the United States, tax legislation and a spate of rulings from other governmental agencies continue to challenge corporate boards to make shareholder interests their top priority.

There is no doubt that U.S. companies are on the right track. Aside from being the most productive in the world, American companies and the performance-based pay that increasingly fuels them are the best hope for steady job creation and economic security during both one's working and retirement years. After all, which would you rather have — your pension plan secured by the American stock market or by the Japanese stock market?

Are CEO pay levels too high? Has the United States been successful in linking executive pay to stock performance? Does executive stock ownership make a difference? Are U.S. executive pay practices better than or worse than international models? What lessons can be drawn from how we pay executives, and how can we apply them to the workforce at large? Should we continue to link CEO pay to performance and can we tie all employees' pay to strategic business objectives? Let's start with pay for performance.

CHAPTER 1

Is There Pay for Performance?

No shareholder initiative has a more direct impact
on shareholder value than [CEO] compensation.

— Institutional Shareholder Services

Lawrence M. Coss was a virtual unknown until the spring of 1996. That is when he landed for the second year in a row at the top of the "highest paid CEO" lists compiled by the major business magazines in the United States. Coss, chairman of Green Tree Financial Corp. in St. Paul, Minnesota, garnered $65.6 million in 1995 — "a tidy sum," as *Business Week* put it, "for a CEO of a consumer-finance company with net income of only $254 million." But the magazine hastened to add that Green Tree's performance was stellar: Its market value had grown to $3.6 billion from $330 million over the previous five years. Earnings per share had grown at an annual rate of 44 percent since 1990.

Coss's compensation is a good example of how pay for performance should work. Five years ago, Green Tree directors set Coss's annual base salary at only $400,000. They linked his bonus — paid largely in company stock — directly to Green Tree's pre-tax earnings. As income rose, so did Coss's pay. "The only way Larry could get substantial compensation was to deliver outstanding performance," Robert S. Nickoloff, chairman of Green Tree's compensation committee, told *Business Week*. "He did, and the performance he delivered went up beyond anyone's expectations."

Further, the 3,000 employees who helped Coss profit on loans for mobile homes, motorcycles and home improvements also shared the wealth. Some 118 executives and managers divided a $7.2 million bonus pool in 1995, while the remaining 2,300 employees each received an extra month's pay that cost the company an additional $3.5 million.

Coss was one of 800 U.S. chief executives who made $1 million or more in 1995, according to *Business Week* data — an "unconscionable" sum, many critics declare, in the face of mammoth downsizings and wages for surviving workers that fail to keep pace with inflation. But such criticism must be tempered by the fact that the Standard & Poor's 500 stock index jumped 37 percent in 1995, and corporate profits rose a hefty 15 percent. Indeed, *Forbes* discovered that the median compensation in 1995 for the chief executives of 800 major U.S. corporations was $1.5 million, a 15 percent rise over 1994 — hardly a dramatic surge in light of stock market performance. The increase was about in line, the magazine noted, with the pay of top-earning physicians, attorneys, fashion models and television personalities.

To be fair, the criticism over "skyrocketing" executive pay does not focus solely on success at the top but also on failure to share the wealth with employees at the bottom and middle. CEO pay at major companies rose 92 percent between 1990 and 1995, according to *Business Week*, while corporate profits swelled 75 percent. In contrast, all worker pay during the same period increased only 16 percent. Clearly, performance-based pay should be distributed evenly. And just as clearly, stock option grants alone should not be the sole component of a chief executive's stock incentive package, since they do not carry the same risk as stock ownership. This is one of the main reasons we advocate purchases of stock as well as stock option awards.

COMPENSATION MOTIVATES PERFORMANCE

However, there is compelling statistical and anecdotal evidence that executive compensation programs strongly motivate CEOs and their senior executives to improve corporate performance. The studies we and others have conducted show a strong correlation between changes in pay and changes in corporate performance. The theory is clear: As investors have demanded greater accountability and returns for their money, boards of directors have forged better links between executive pay and performance, largely by shifting more pay into stock options and ownership. (See Appendix A for a discussion of the types of long-term incentives used to reward top managers.)

Nonetheless, many critics of executive compensation argue that there is only a modest link between a company's performance and the compensation of its chief executive officer. The most well known of these critics is Graef S. "Bud" Crystal, a widely quoted, former executive compensation consultant and now a journalist and professor. As publisher of *The Crystal Report*, he documents examples of companies and industries that show very little pay for performance. For example, in the July 1995 issue, *The Crystal*

Report evaluated 424 large-market capitalization firms, comparing the CEO's base salary, total cash compensation (salary plus bonus) and total direct compensation, or TDC (total cash compensation plus the value of stock plans, particularly stock options at grant), to the size and performance of the company. In evaluating TDC, *The Crystal Report* found that only one-third of the variation in TDC could be explained by company size, performance (shareholder returns) and CEO tenure, leaving fully two-thirds unexplained. The study concluded that there is limited pay for performance.

One could have a Talmudic level of debate over methodologies without a resolution. However, a few points should be made:

- *The Crystal Report* has been studying this issue for years, and the amount of pay for performance has increased substantially over time. In fact, Bud Crystal should be congratulated for part of this improvement, since he has been such an articulate critic over the past decade and has in fact influenced the legislative efforts impacting executive pay.

- The primary dispute relates to the TDC definition, including the *hypothetical grant value of options*, or "grant valuation" approach, which uses the Black-Scholes option valuation method (see Appendix B). While all compensation experts agree that option grants have *economic* value (even at grant, when most have no intrinsic profit built in), we disagree that it is appropriate to correlate this hypothetical *future* value with *past* financial performance. This is explored further below.

Our own studies of top management compensation, as well as numerous academic studies, show a very different finding. In Figure 1-1, Watson Wyatt's 1996 – 97 survey of top management compensation shows first that total cash compensation for CEOs, which is their base salary plus bonus, is indeed sensitive to the stock market performance of their companies in terms of Total Return to Shareholders, or TRS. TRS is defined as the annualized stock price appreciation plus dividends, divided by the company's beginning stock price five years earlier. In some cases, CEO cash compensation drops steeply when performance declines. While the average CEO received a nine percent increase in cash compensation in 1995, those at companies where shareholder return was below the median (but still positive) had no increase at all in total cash. This finding continues the trend toward increased sensitivity about pay and performance that began in the early 1990s. On the other

Figure 1-1: Changes in Pay are Sensitive to Changes in Performance

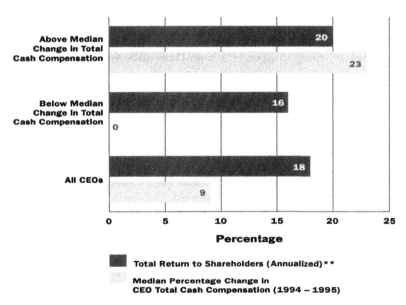

* Total Cash Compensation = Base salary + bonus and/or other cash

**Five-Year Total Return to Shareholders (TRS)
(TRS = Stock price appreciation + dividends ÷ beginning stock price)

Source: Watson Wyatt study of 398 large public companies with CEOs with more than five years of tenure as CEO.

hand, companies experiencing a 20 percent increase in TRS (equal to $1 billion or more in many instances) increased their CEOs' total cash compensation by 23 percent.

We then looked at TDC. However, our definition did not use the *hypothetical future value* of the options but the *historical actual value*.[1] Our data show that those companies with the highest paid CEOs out-performed the lowest paid ones in many industries (see Figure 1-2). For all 398 companies in our study, companies that paid CEOs at a higher-than-median level registered nearly seven percentage points higher in terms of TRS. For large capitalization companies, this difference can mean hundreds of millions of dollars of increased shareholder value. Since much of the pay was delivered via exercised stock options, companies appear to be directly linking executive and shareholder interests. While it is impossible to say with certainty that the higher pay opportunity *caused* the better stock performance, there is a strong statistical relationship. Most importantly, such an outcome is so favorable to shareholders that it is certainly worth the risk. We believe that this difference in

Figure 1-2: High-Performing Companies Pay Better Than Lower Performing Companies

CEO Pay*	Amount	Annualized TRS**
High	$3.4 million	21%
Low	$1.1 million	14%

* 1995 salary + bonus + other cash compensation + profit from stock options exercised + restricted stock grants
High = Above the median; Low = Below the median

**Five-Year Total Return to Shareholders (TRS)
(TRS = Stock price appreciation + dividends ÷ beginning stock price)

Source: Watson Wyatt study of 398 large public companies with CEOs with more than five years of tenure as CEO.

1 Salary + bonus + stock option profits + restricted stock grants.

methodologies — *theoretical grant value* of options *versus actual historical value, each of which is then compared to historical TRS* — explains some of the differences in findings among the various studies.

A grant of stock options, it must be remembered, does not guarantee a big payoff. To show what we mean, take two companies, Growco and Stodgeco, each with different histories, strategies, products and management styles, but with an identical goal to increase TRS. The CEOs of each company are granted 500,000 stock options (with proportional grants for other employees), each at the fair market value of, say, $20 for both companies, and each with a Black-Scholes value on their options of $10 (see Appendix B), for a hypothetical grant value of $5 million. Over the next year, Growco performs brilliantly, partly due to luck and partly due to an excellent strategy and execution. Its stock price rises fivefold, to $100, and the CEO realizes $40 million in pre-tax option profits. During that same year, Stodgeco poorly executes a flawed strategy and experiences some bad luck (price war, bad weather, loss in a lawsuit, etc.). Its stock price plunges to $11, and it becomes a takeover target. Naturally, the Stodgeco CEO's stock options are worthless.

As we look back on these two companies and perform our statistical analysis, what can we conclude?

1. The highly paid Growco CEO worked for a company that performed substantially better than the lower paid CEO.

2. Stock options or any incentive plan are no guarantee of success for shareholders. Overall strategy execution is essential.

3. Stock options are a relatively low-risk form of compensation, since they pay off handsomely for success and not at all for failure.

4. The Stodgeco CEO did not walk off with nothing. It is very likely he received a competitive salary and benefits, which we favor, despite his company's poor performance. It is important, however, to structure salary and benefits so that they do not diminish the motivational impact of a stock option program, because stock options have the highest probability of driving a successful strategy. In this case, total pay for performance eventually wins the day, because the Stodgeco CEO probably lost his job because of poor strategy and execution.

5. Those executive pay experts *who value options at grant* would have completely missed the boat on this one. Their analysis would have valued the two option grants at about $5 million for each CEO (500,000 x $10 estimated per option value). The one-year look-back using the "grant valuation" approach would have shown two identically paid CEOs, one of whose companies performed in a stellar manner and one of whom performed terribly. They would have concluded that there is no pay for performance. They would, of course, have been wrong. To be fair, Bud Crystal occasionally studies stock option grants and subsequent stock price increases *over time* for the same individuals. He typically finds no pay for performance using this method as well. His explanation usually relates to the timing of option grants and stock price fluctuations. The timing of option grants can clearly have a major impact on their ultimate value. Nevertheless, the primary studies that critics use are indeed the intercompany comparisons as described above.

6. However, we still cannot conclude that the high pay opportunity *caused* the high performance. Might Growco's stock have gone to $100 if the CEO had been granted only 100,000 stock

options, or even none? Of course, this question is impossible to answer, but we have come full circle: Is it worth the risk that the board would take on behalf of shareholders? In this simplistic example, the answer is obviously yes. Real life, however, is much more complex. But what is the policy alternative for the board? Follow the Japanese or German model of no stock option grants for executives? That model has not worked for the Japanese, and we believe it certainly would not work in the United States, either, in today's globally competitive economy.

This methodological dispute is not just an arcane argument among experts, but rather it defines the nature of the argument. Specifically, if the entire stock market goes down, and if companies continue to grant stock options, the grant methodology will show even lower linkages of pay to performance. Our methodology, as seen in the example, should show ever-rising links, even as pay declines with the market.

REAL-LIFE EXAMPLES OF PAY FOR PERFORMANCE

We have shown that there is a fairly strong statistical relationship between pay and performance. But how does this happen? The reality is that this occurs one CEO, one company, one board, one compensation committee at a time. It takes some kind of incentive plan to be developed, a stock option grant to be sized and made, and a conversation to take place between the compensation committee or its chair and the individual CEO.

If there is indeed no pay for performance in U.S. board rooms, a compensation committee at an under-performing company would say something like this to its CEO:

"We know you tried, and you had bad luck. We want you to stay anyway. We have looked at competitive data, and we need to pay you above the market to keep you. Here is a large bonus."

But this is not happening!

What really happens goes something like this:

"This is a pay-for-performance company. We know you and your team worked hard, but some things didn't work out and you had bad luck. We will continue to grant options to you, but we will decrease your annual incentive this year and you will not get any salary increase. We also will implement stock ownership guidelines and we will make it easier for you to buy stock. Your old stock options could be valuable, because they have seven (eight, nine) years left before they must be exercised. Good luck."

My colleagues and I at Watson Wyatt have attended hundreds of compensation committee meetings. We have never heard, "Profits went down and pay went up." Instead, our discussions with boards of directors and their chief executives involve ways to properly reward and motivate the CEO and the top management team, and thereby enrich the shareholders if they are successful.

The following two anecdotes describe the process more fully. Company names and some of the facts have been changed to protect client confidentiality.

HEALTH CARE COMPANY: A BOOM GONE BUST

In the early 1990s, a health care company was anticipating dramatic growth in size, profitability and TRS. The CEO had basically built this company from scratch, doing a terrific job building up the organization through organic growth and acquisitions. Stock price at the time was around $15 a share, and the market capitalization was around $500 million. This CEO anticipated dramatic growth in the demand for the kind of health care services his company provided. He expected the stock price to double or triple in the next two to three years. What could we do to make sure he shared extremely well in this growth? The 50,000 to 100,000 stock options he had been getting every year did not begin to capture the upside opportunity he wanted.

We recommended a *premium-priced stock option*, which has an exercise price higher than today's stock market price. If the exercise price was 50 percent higher than the current $15 per share, or $22.50, and if the CEO did not take any additional stock options for five years, the board could be justified in awarding *one million stock options* in a lump sum grant today. That way, if the stock price tripled to $45, the CEO would make a $22.50 profit per share on one million options, or $22.5 million. That was exactly what he had in mind, and the board and shareholders approved the plan.

However, when President Clinton was elected in 1992, many of the proposed changes in health care reform were extremely damaging to this company. Instead of rising, the stock price fell by half, to around $7 or $8. Those stock options were now about $15 out of the money, or "underwater." It was not for lack of strategy, but the company certainly had bad luck. The health care market moved out from under it, which caused the stock market to do the same. Subsequently, the CEO became chairman, and the company brought in another CEO, who is in the process of turning the company around. The stock price is now back to $15 or $16, and the company uses more traditional stock options now.

It remains to be seen whether the premium options will ever be valuable, although it is doubtful. These options will probably expire before they are valuable. Clearly, a large stock option grant is no guarantee of success.

CHEMICAL COMPANY: FROM BUST TO BOOM

Another client is a multi-billion-dollar chemical company. Its new CEO felt that the company's costs were bloated and that it had diversified inappropriately. He believed that there was a real opportunity to increase shareholder value substantially by streamlining the organization and selling business units. Anticipating that outcome, he wanted a plan for himself and his top management team where they would continue to get stock options, but more importantly, they would buy a great deal of stock at a small discount. After receiving approval, they bought millions of shares of stock at a 15 percent discount using pre-tax dollars. They used what we call a Management Stock Purchase Plan (see Chapter 6). The CEO also converted his Supplemental Executive Retirement Plan (SERP) to stock. He then proceeded to implement his strategy to good effect. The chemical industry, which had been going through some down years, began moving back up again, so he had a combination of good luck and good execution of strategy. The company's stock went from $25 a share to $125 a share, a five-fold increase. The CEO's net worth went from a few million dollars to around $50 million. Today, the company is considered one of the great success stories in the chemical industry.

REAL-LIFE CONCLUSIONS

Our lessons from these two anecdotes are basically identical to the conclusions derived from statistical evidence.

First and most critically, an incentive plan, no matter how perfectly structured, is not an answer to bad luck, a change in the marketplace that is outside the company's control, a poor strategy or even a great strategy poorly executed. Compensation is only one of the management tools necessary for creating value for the company.

Second, it is important to measure the risk. In the health care company, the CEO received one million options. Yes, that created some potential dilution. But that is a relatively low-cost way to fund a program like this. Because of bad luck and the execution of the strategy, those options are worthless to him, so there was no payment made and no significant risk. With the chemical company, the executives purchased huge amounts of stock at a small discount, which is an additional cost to the company, but it worked out extremely well.

From a policy perspective, a board or shareholder needs to ask, "Is it worth the risk? Are we comfortable offering these programs to our executives with the hope of motivating them to execute the right strategies? Is it worth giving the top managers one or two or three percent of the increase in market value to see if those strategies will be implemented?"

The answer is clearly yes. In the case of the health care company, would the shareholders have preferred the scenario that actually happened — the stock price falling? Or would they have preferred the stock price to triple to $45 so that they all would have owned a $1.5 billion company, while the CEO earned $22.5 million for such an impressive performance? Again, the answers are obvious.

HOW HIGH IS HIGH?

Of course, there will always be CEOs whose pay is not justified by their performance. And the protracted market boom leaves some chief executives perched atop mountains of potential fortunes in terms of restricted shares whose value may not match the CEO's performance. On balance, however, while total CEO compensation is high by "regular people's" standards, it is at a suitable level given the risks under which CEOs operate and the tremendous value they can create.

One factor to keep in mind is that executive pay broadly reflects a company's size. Larger and more complex organizations are generally required to pay more to attract executives with the appropriate experience to manage them. Figure 1-3 delineates average CEO compensation by size of company. CEOs at larger companies have much higher pay — and more "at risk" compensation — than those at smaller companies. On average, however, the CEO position at most companies is highly leveraged, i.e., incentives such as cash and stock are a rising proportion of total pay.

Figure 1-3: Average CEO Compensation by Revenue Size (All industries except financial)

Company Revenue	Base Salary (000)	Bonus Amount (000)	Bonus % of Salary	Total Cash Comp. (000)	Average Stock Option Grant* (000)
Below $100 Million	$202.1	$103.1	51	$261.4	$410.2
$100 Million to $500 Million	$316.6	$191.2	60	$449.0	$725.1
Over $500 Million to $1 Billion	$416.6	$303.1	73	$628.1	$689.8
Above $1 Billion	$624.9	$451.6	72	$1,017.7	$2,227.2

* The option grants represent a subset of the larger database and are calculated by multiplying the number of options granted by the exercise price.

Source: Watson Wyatt Data Services.

Another way to evaluate executive pay is to compare the highest paid CEOs relative to the highest paid athletes and entertainers. Figure 1-4 indicates that while the Top 10 CEOs earned multi-million-dollar compensation in 1995, the top entertainers fared considerably better, and the top athletes did not do badly, either. Oprah Winfrey earned more than the top four CEOs combined. Boxer Mike Tyson, as *Forbes* noted, earned the first $1 billion hourly fee in history: $25 million for 89 seconds of work knocking out Peter McNeeley at the MGM Grand in Las Vegas. On average, top-athlete and top-CEO salaries seem comparable, but do Riddick Bowe or Shaquille O'Neal add as much economic value to the world and create as many jobs as the CEO of General Electric, who also earned $22 million?

The American public, it seems, asks the same question. In a recent Roper Center survey, higher percentages of those polled said that athletes (90 percent), entertainers (86 percent) and attorneys (86 percent) were overpaid than said the same of CEOs of major corporations.

Figure 1-4: 1995 Pay Levels for Selected
Occupations ($ in millions)

Rank	CEOs		Entertainers		Athletes	
1	Green Tree	$65	O. Winfrey	$171	M. Jordan	$44
2	Travelers	50	S. Spielberg	150	M. Tyson	40
3	G.E.	22	The Beatles	130	D. Sanders	22
4	Amgen	21	M. Jackson	90	R. Bowe	22
5	DSC Comns.	19	Rolling Stones	77	S. O'Neal	22
6	U.S. Robotics	18	Eagles	75	G. Foreman	18
7	Andrew Corp.	17	A. Schwarzenegger	74	A. Agassi	16
8	Forest Labs	17	D. Copperfield	74	J. Nicklaus	15
9	Goodyear	16	J. Carrey	63	M. Schumacher	15
10	Sears	16	M. Crichton	59	W. Gretzky	14
Average		$26		$96		$23

Sources: Business Week, Forbes.

The chief executive cannot have a bad season, trip or stumble in a game without paying a heavy price. More than ever, the CEO is likely to lose his job when he does not deliver the profits shareholders expect. No less august companies than IBM, General Motors and American Express have replaced under-performing CEOs in recent years. Indeed, 10 to 20 percent of major companies' CEOs change every year. Just since 1993, according to *Forbes*, the median number of years a chief executive stays in the job has shrunk from five years to three in the largest industrial companies. And when a CEO falls from grace, he is not just off the team, he is out of the game. While a CEO can receive a very generous severance package, once he has been removed, he can often be unemployable.

Another point of comparison with CEO pay is the compensation of investment bankers. While their pay is not generally made public, it is common knowledge that top-ranking bankers earn between $30 million and $50 million per year, and their average cash compensation is between $15 million and $20 million. Again, while an individual merger and acquisition expert can play an important (and controversial) role in the U.S. economy, he or she does not create the value nor the jobs of a chief executive officer.

In sum, the value U.S. society imputes to CEOs, as evidenced by their compensation, is certainly not out of line with these other occupations. Of the $1 trillion in value created by the U.S. stock market in 1995, the CEOs of all *Fortune 500* companies were paid only a fraction of this increase — about $1 billion (.1%). To put the comparison on an individual level, the controversial Albert J. Dunlap's two-year tenure as CEO of Scott Paper Co. earned him $100 million, a figure lambasted by the media. However, the company's stock price rose 225 percent, to a market value of $6.5 billion, making Dunlap's compensation less than two percent of the wealth he helped to create — good value by anyone's standards. Further, his move to Sunbeam caused that company's stock price to rise 52 percent — or $521 million — in one day, one of the biggest gains prompted by a CEO announcement for a single trading session in New York Stock Exchange history. In this instance, Dunlap's track record was so solid that he did not even have to perform to earn his pay.

WHY IS CEO PAY SO HIGH?

There is no doubt that executive pay has risen faster than average employee earnings. Bud Crystal estimates that the typical head of a large American corporation earned total compensation (excluding perquisites and fringe benefits) around 40 times the pay of an average manufacturing worker in 1974. Today, however, that multiple has risen to 225. Frederic W. Cook, another executive compensation consultant, disagrees with Crystal's pay differential, arguing that it has merely doubled over the past 20 years — from about 30 to 1 in 1974 to 60 to 1 in 1994. Higher ratios like Crystal's, he points out, are based on average CEO compensation in the 300 largest market-capitalized companies in the United States and on average production workers' compensation. "The largest corporations do not represent your typical corporation," he argues, "and hourly paid production workers, while important, do not represent your typical employee."

Regardless of which figures you use, it is clear that executive pay has grown faster than the rate of inflation (three to four percent) and faster than average employee increases (two to three percent or less).

But these increases must be kept in perspective. During the 1990s, CEO pay, including option grants, has grown 12 to 15 percent annually, but NASDAQ stock prices have grown 20 percent per year over the same period.

Higher CEO pay can be explained by a number of factors:

1) **A scarcity of talent creates "bidding wars."** Boards of directors will pay what seem to be eyebrow-raising sums for the proven ability of a CEO to add tens of millions of dollars to a company's profit each year. Even though there are occasional, and conspicuous, performance failures, as former Harvard president Derek Bok points out in *The Cost of Talent,* we cannot support his more general claim that the competitive system itself was corroded by the free-market values of the Reagan administration in the 1980s. (Surely Bok would not ascribe the remarkable rise of the stock-rich Harvard endowment during his tenure — from $1 billion in 1971 to $5 billion in 1990 — to money-squandering CEOs.) Instead, we agree with economists Robert H. Frank and Philip J. Cook, who argue in *The Winner-Take-All Society* that "the explosion of CEO pay has resulted not from any imperfections in competitive forces but rather from their increasing intensity."

CEO promotions from within — the most common choice for decades — are being balanced by boards searching outside their own companies for the talent needed to downsize, restructure and globalize their operations. Frank and Cook's study of CEOs hired by 800 of the largest U.S. manufacturing and service companies show that the number of new CEOs who had been with their companies for less than three years grew by almost 50 percent from the early 1970s to the 1990s. Not only must boards now pay premiums to woo candidates away from other firms, they also must pay more to their most valued senior officers to keep them from jumping ship. Of course, once the first seven-figure (or eight-figure) compensation package is inked, Frank and Cook note, "it becomes a benchmark that makes subsequent multi-million-dollar packages much easier to justify."

A comparison of CEO pay with directors' pay offers further evidence that a limited *supply* of qualified CEO candidates drives up their price. Directors' pay has risen nearly 10 percent per year for the past 5 years, according to the Watson Wyatt Directors Survey, but it has not gone up nearly as rapidly as CEO pay over the same time period. Upon first glance, the pool of talent available to boards is somewhat similar to that available to CEOs. But close inspection reveals that it is a very different pool. Many more people are available to become board members, which explains why the pay increases have been so much lower. The supply of CEOs, on the other hand, is much smaller. They must not only have the broad corporate experience and judgment of a board member, they also must possess the leadership and vision to guide 10,000; 50,000; 100,000 or even 500,000 employees. It is a much smaller pool. Because the even smaller subset of successful CEOs creates so much more value, the CEOs are worth more. It is a prudent risk for a board to offer $5- to $10-million packages (mostly stock options) to increase the probability of a $1- to $5-billion increase in market value.

2) A "winner-take-all" mentality has invaded the executive suite. While the broad employee population contributes mightily to corporate success, CEOs and their senior management teams are of critical importance and work under more intense pressure

than ever before. The high debt that many companies are still working off from the 1980s, combined with rapid change and keen competition in global markets, makes the CEO's job critical and fraught with risk. The board's job is to find the candidate whose enthusiasm for assuming risk is in direct proportion to the value he or she can create. In a limited universe of truly well-qualified candidates, boards and CEO candidates alike ultimately find themselves asking, "Is it worth the risk?" High compensation packages frequently provide the answer. And as we have noted earlier, CEOs who fail to perform well find themselves out the door quickly, which mitigates the risk for shareholders.

This is the typical American scenario, where the position of chief executive officer has become more powerful and strategic than ever before. The CEO sits squarely where the buck stops. In other cultures, however, the situation is different. In Japan and Germany, the function is much more team-oriented, which provides the advantage of more people sharing the accountability. But this structure provides an equally strong disadvantage: Far fewer lightning-quick strategic thrusts and changes in direction can occur when a large team, rather than one person supported by a team, is making those decisions. Such a high-risk, high-reward framework should be compensated.

Frank and Cook argue that their winner-take-all market creates its own set of social problems by attracting excess talent from other fields. Certainly, more of the rewards of a successful corporation need to be shared with large groups of employees. However, the CEO provides the dominant leadership.

3) **The stigma of making unpopular decisions needs to be compensated.** A CEO's decision to downsize the workforce, shutter factories or discontinue product lines is often unpopular

with employees, communities and the press. As CEOs become more well known in society — indeed, become celebrities to some extent — they risk an increasing amount of vilification. CEOs need to be compensated in part for that stigma. While this may appear mercenary, it is clear that companies — or even countries — that do not compensate for this stigma effect end up with bloated payrolls.

Of course, another way to gain perspective on the CEO pay multiple is to ask why worker pay has been so flat. An increasingly global economy is one answer. With companies driven to cut costs to remain competitive, many use cheaper offshore workers, which decreases the demand for highly paid U.S. workers. As we will discuss later, such a global labor market does not really exist yet for CEOs — and certainly not for those from developing nations. Moreover, many well-paying manufacturing jobs no longer exist in a rising information-based service economy. Because of these fundamental changes, the influence of unions has waned as their membership has declined. Another possible answer to the conundrum of slow-rising employee pay has to do with the large amount of immigration that the United States has experienced. Many experts argue that this increased supply of labor — while good overall for the economy — can help to keep wages from rising rapidly. This is not to say that workers and managers cannot or should not share the rewards of senior management's good, well-executed strategy. In many companies they do already, with performance-based compensation supplementing salaries and hourly wages. Just as with CEOs, there is a drive to make pay more commensurate with performance. Compensation plans designed to reward all employees in proportion to their contributions are excellent ways to moderate concerns about pay inequities.

But rather than ask whether CEO pay is too high, it is more pertinent to ask whether a CEO would have done as good a job for a $50 million compensation package as for a $100 million plan. The answer is probably yes. But motivation is an art, not an exact science. The purpose of an incentive package is to motivate stellar performance from top executives on behalf of their shareholders. It is impossible to know precisely how large an incentive must be up front to produce a certain effect.

Compensation committees work very hard to achieve the right combination of risk and reward. For example, look at some of the major turnarounds that have occurred in the 1990s — Sears, Goodyear, IBM, Travelers and many others — turnarounds in which anywhere from $5 billion to $20 billion or more in value has been created. In order to motivate a new CEO to change a company's strategy fundamentally, compensation committees have to award options worth one or two percent of that upside appreciation, or $200 million (at 1 percent) on a $20 billion increase in share value. That sounds like a lot of money, and it is, but it pales in comparison to the amount that stockholders receive — $19.8 billion. Compensation committees also have to include some floor level of compensation in order to hire a new CEO. This protection usually takes the form of a few million dollars in salary and guaranteed bonus. Again, this is a lot of money, but it is also a very prudent investment for the shareholders to undertake to see if they can achieve $10 billion or $20 billion in appreciation.

More often than not, these compensation packages do motivate financial turnarounds. It is interesting to speculate why these new CEOs have the wherewithal to create the turnarounds. After all, the "failed" CEO typically also had a pay-for-performance package.

Is it simply that the newly recruited CEO has so much more upside opportunity than the prior CEO? While the higher leverage is part of the answer, we also believe that the new CEO has a different charter. In addition, the new CEO is not wedded to the former strategy and management team. He or she has the clean slate and economic incentives to overcome the stigma and create a new team and a new strategy.

INTERNATIONAL EXECUTIVE COMPENSATION

Much also has been made of high pay for American CEOs compared to their counterparts in Europe and Japan. Pay multiples on the order of 17 to 35 have been quoted for CEOs of major Japanese, French, German and British firms, compared to multiples of more than 200 for U.S. chief executives. In reality, however, these are like comparisons of sushi, bratwurst and steak: all mouth-watering but actually inappropriate or irrelevant. The direct importing of Japanese or German "compensation philosophies" into the United States is as unlikely to work as the exporting of American programs to those countries. However, we should all examine each other's programs for value. Just as the United States has learned much about management from abroad — worker cooperation, just-in-time inventories, quality, etc. — so should other nations explore U.S. management programs, particularly compensation.

One major problem with international comparisons of CEO compensation is the vastly different size of the countries and corporations being compared. The U.S. economy is twice as large as the next largest, Japan, and three to five times as large as the economies of Western Europe. Similarly, the market value of companies in each of those countries varies greatly in size. Figure 1-5 brings the contrast to life. The 10th-largest company in Japan,

Figure 1-5: Market Value of the Tenth-Largest Industrial Company ($ in billions)

Country	Market Value of Tenth-Largest Company	Percentage of U.S.
United States	60.2	100
Japan	37.0	62
Germany	14.5	24
France	10.6	18
United Kingdom	20.0	33
Italy	4.8	8
Sweden	4.1	7

Source: Business Week.

as measured by its market value, is only two-thirds as large as the 10th-largest American corporation. The 10th-largest company in Great Britain, as measured by market value, is only one-third the size of the comparable American firm. Since executives at large corporations are paid more than those at smaller companies — logical and defensible, as they have more responsibility and risk — and since the United States has so many large companies, it explains part of the higher pay multiple for U.S. CEOs.

A number of other factors also make it difficult to compare CEO compensation across borders. Unlike the U.S. market, there is limited competition for executive talent in many international markets. Promotions are made largely from within; lifetime employment, especially in Japan, is the respected order of business. There is no need, then, to pay a premium for a particular executive's services because he has no place else to go. Fundamentally, the labor market for executives in the United States is very large, robust and liquid, typical indicators of a healthy, dynamic market.

International comparisons also do not account for differences in local welfare benefits, tax rates and cultural values. The CEO of a Japanese company employing more than 3,000 employees earned an average of $440,000 before taxes, according to a 1995 Watson Wyatt study. However, many enjoyed "benefits in kind," such as foreign holidays, golf club memberships (wildly expensive in Japan), subsidized housing, transportation to the office, large entertainment expense accounts and more.

Further, the marginal tax rate in Japan is 65 percent, causing Japanese executives to attempt to shift compensation from their own tax return to the corporation's. In evaluating the job in design *per se*, a Japanese CEO's job is also very different from an American CEO's. In general, a Japanese executive does not have the same responsibilities or direct involvement with the management of the enterprise that an American executive does. One can argue, therefore, that the job is worth less to the corporation.

Cultural differences factor into pay for performance as well. Companies in Japan and Germany, for instance, pursue a broad range of social objectives in addition to profits for shareholders. In Japan, chief executives are expected to be loyal to the other members of their *keiretsu*, or enterprise group, regardless of the impact on their company. German CEOs are supposed to be paid a performance-related bonus — up to one-third of their salary — but the relationship between pay and performance, we have found, is not as rigorous as it is in the United States. German bonuses can be generous even when the firm does not do well.

A larger issue here is whether American executives and shareholders have a different time horizon than their counterparts in Japan and continental Europe. Critics believe that U.S. companies are too short-sighted ("myopic") and that executives in other parts of the world take a longer-term view for both their investments and their returns to shareholders.

This issue is another one of the great mythologies of executive compensation. There is virtually no evidence that either the U.S. stock market or American executives are myopic. Quite the contrary. There is much evidence to show that if longer-term investments are made in the United States, the stock market will reward those companies handsomely by increasing their stock prices. Executives need to be rewarded and have their reward programs aligned optimally with both short- and long-term investments.

Finally, the way pay is *set* outside the United States can have a decided affect on how much it relates to executive performance. In Germany, the pay of the chief executive (head of the management board) is established by a supervisory board, often chaired by the company's previous CEO. In addition, companies tend to be loosely joined by interlocking relationships among companies, banks and governments, which lowers the risk — and pay — for the top job. The problem is arguably even more complex in Japan, where the web of cross-shareholdings is far more extensive and tangled, and bosses are often overseen only by other bosses. In such a situation it is terribly difficult to associate pay directly with performance. As an article in *The Economist* concludes, "The vast international disparities in executive pay reflect the fact that pay is still largely a national matter." Nevertheless, as we shall see, some convergence is beginning.

All of these issues are mostly beside the point, however. Executives outside the United States and Great Britain, particularly those in Germany and Japan, do not have the incentives to create shareowner value. It is true that U.S. CEOs earn substantially more than their international counterparts. But U.S. shareholders appear much better off for that investment.

Interestingly, compensation packages for European CEOs, especially those in Great Britain, are looking more and more like their counterparts in the United States. We believe it is these programs in the United Kingdom that have helped its economy and the stock market performance of its major companies. Stock options are being added to base salaries, and corporate performance is improving. Of course, total compensation is rising substantially as well (along with public outcries, changes in corporate governance and media criticism). But the fact that British executive compensation is being modeled on U.S. pay packages indicates that the United States must be doing something right. In fact, as in the United States, Great Britain has been looking into executive pay, performance and institutional ownership. As in the United States, institutional owners want to be sure they are getting their money's worth.

OTHER IMPORTANT ISSUES

The United States is, indeed, doing many things right when it rewards top managers on the basis of their performance. In addition to doing well for their shareholders, chief executives also have performed well for their workforces, despite assertions that rising corporate profits have come unfairly at the expense of employees.

The fact is, workers are not worse off now than they were in 1979. The share of corporate revenue going to employees has remained constant ever since World War II, while the share going to profits is actually low by postwar standards. As Figure 1-6 shows, employee compensation as a share of national income actually has risen slightly since 1950. Meanwhile, corporate profits as a share of national income have declined slowly but steadily over the same period and have yet to regain the near-20 percent mark they hit after World War II.

Figure 1-6: Corporate Profits and Private Industry Employee Compensation as a Share of National Income

Source: Department of Commerce, Bureau of Economic Analysis.

What *has* changed in all-employee pay is the mix of cash wages and non-cash benefits. The latter now account for 41 percent of compensation, *versus* 20 percent in the 1950s, according to the Employment Policy Foundation of Washington, D.C. Figure 1-7 demonstrates the situation. Using the study's terminology, real (after inflation) hourly earnings have declined from their peak in the mid-1970s, but real hourly compensation (including benefits) is at its highest level ever. When the mix of compensation between cash wages and non-cash benefits changes over time, with the relative share of benefits rising, increases in real wages will underestimate increases in workers' well-being. Average family income is another indicator of all-employee well-being. This measure stood at $51,000 for 1995, according to *Fortune* — an $11,000 inflation-adjusted increase from the 1960s. By these standards, CEOs have performed well for their employees.

Figure 1-7: Private Industry Employee Earnings and Compensation (1959=100)

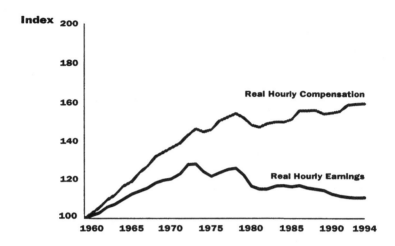

Source: Department of Labor, Bureau of Labor Statistics.

U.S. productivity has also undergone fundamental improvement, thanks to top management's emphasis on re-engineering, streamlining and downsizing — activities undertaken to improve corporate performance and market value. Output per worker is rising at a 1.1 percent annual rate, about the same as in the 1980s. But this figure does not include data from the information economy, sure to show a higher rate of growth once the Commerce Department revises productivity statistics later in the decade. Moreover, as of this writing, real corporate profits have risen by 34 percent since 1992 — a bigger increase than they registered during the previous 15 years — without significant price increases. Higher profits, in turn, have sent the stock market soaring since 1992, a big benefit for employees who own stock on their own or through 401(k) plans and ESOPs and for investors at large. Further, this increase in value has made pensions more secure as well.

There is no doubt that the great success of many American corporations, at least in part, reflects the compensation plan that spurs their CEOs to achieve higher levels of performance to gain higher rewards. The clear winner in such a scenario, of course, is the shareowner, for whom the CEO acts as agent. Less clear winners, but also substantially benefited, are the employees who work on the shareholders' behalf, as we shall see in the next chapter.

CHAPTER 2

We All Benefit When CEOs Perform

It may not be a good place to work, but it's a helluva stock to own.

— Laid-off insurance company employee

When that employee talked to *Business Week* for a 1996 cover story on "Economic Anxiety," he had worked for Travelers Corp. for 29 years before taking a severance package from the Hartford insurer at the end of 1994. Since then, the shares he still owns in the company have doubled in value. This did not change the *social* impact of his layoff, but it certainly changed the economics!

In the course of downsizing their workforces and streamlining their operations to become more competitive, CEOs and their executive teams have added billions of dollars to their companies' value, rewarding their shareholders with higher stock prices and themselves with stock option profits. In the past, improved returns for shareholders were typically associated with growing incomes for everyone. Is this still true? Brookings Institution senior fellow Margaret M. Blair argues in *The Brookings Review*, "jackpot compensation awards to executives are coming just as the earnings potential and job security of the average working person seem weaker than at any time in the past 40 years."

But the astute reader will note that just six months after *Business Week* ran its cover story on "Economic Anxiety," it followed up with a shorter article called "Whatever Happened to Economic Anxiety?" in which it heralded "the best labor market in decades." The percentage of the civilian population now working is 63 percent, the highest level ever, according to the magazine. Moreover, people are finding positions quickly. Challenger, Gray & Christmas, the Chicago-based outplacement firm, calculates that its clients took only 2.8 months to find new work in late 1996, the least amount of time since the firm began tracking the numbers in the early 1980s.

With overall unemployment rates hovering at five percent and wages finally starting to rise even for manufacturing workers, is it any wonder when the Conference Board reports that consumer confidence is twice as high as it was in 1994? Despite the sometimes shrill and headline-blaring media coverage of CEOs being paid princely sums to throw their loyal "serfs" onto the street, *CEOs and their teams are doing something right.* In fact, they are doing two things *very* right — *providing stronger job security and stronger retirement security. It is one of the great ironies of U.S. executive pay that U.S. CEOs are excoriated for their high pay despite creating phenomenal employment opportunities.* Meanwhile, the world's media are silent about the extraordinarily high unemployment rate (above 10 percent) in Canada, the United Kingdom, France, Ireland, Italy and Germany — despite their relatively low CEO pay!

STRONGER JOB SECURITY

Chief executive officers have promoted stronger job security for those employees who survive the downsizings and other actions taken to make their companies more efficient in order to realize a higher market value. A company better able to withstand competition — and preferably lead its industry into the fray — will always be a far more secure source of continued employment and community support than one that sacrifices profits in the truly short term and ephemeral interest of protecting employees and communities.

It is also important to point out that in addition to changing the strategy, downsizing is one of the key options available to a CEO in order to maximize a company's value. After all, individuals are laid off because their jobs are eliminated. Companies explicitly or implicitly calculate the return from an individual and compare it with their costs (i.e., salary, benefits, etc.). Those individuals or jobs with a negative return are eliminated. Otherwise, keeping those people on the payroll jeopardizes the jobs of the rest of the employees. "Layoffs are crucial to growth," George Gilder, a fellow at the Discovery Institute in Seattle, noted in a *Harper's Magazine* roundtable on the "new capitalism." "The more layoffs in a particular area, the more business starts and the more long-term economic growth. An economy with layoffs is an economy that can create jobs and opportunities."

Stephen Roach, the chief economist at Morgan Stanley, has long been a supporter of the need for U.S. companies to restructure to improve their productivity and competitiveness. He believes that the restructuring of U.S. companies during the 1990s was an extraordinary success. However, in a 1996 seminal article in the *Harvard Business Review*, he argues that the time has come for investment and growth. He believes that at the national and corporate level, this requires an investment in human capital plus R&D. The stock-based incentives that helped propel the restructuring will be useful in motivating the proper decisions for growth. And consistent with Roach's recommendations, stock-based incentives should be applied to all employees, not just executives.

Ultimately, of course, the stock market is the final arbiter of the economic impact of business decisions. Some argue that the market is myopic and fixated on short-term results when it rewards layoff decisions with rising stock prices. But is the market also myopic when it rewards — as it does — long-term investment decisions, such as pharmaceutical R&D and major capital investments, with rising stock prices despite the short-term reduction of earnings? We think CEOs are fully aware of the tradeoffs made by the market. Further, to the extent that a CEO truly jeopardized future value through layoffs, we believe the market would react extremely negatively. CEOs are sensitive to this issue and make layoffs only after extensive analysis. The market has enormous confidence in these decisions. If a group of companies over a period of years made excessive, strategy-damaging layoffs, the market would change its view and react either neutrally or negatively to workforce reductions.

The fact of the matter is that the current economy, despite a number of downsizings, has created a large number of jobs — 46 million — more than it has eliminated since 1970. Many of these jobs have higher pay. More than half of all new jobs between 1983 and 1993 were created in fields with above-average earnings, according to the Committee for Economic Development, a think tank. The years 1994 and 1995 were even better: Two-thirds of new jobs were above the median wage and in high-wage occupations, says Joseph E. Stiglitz, former chairman of President Clinton's Council of Economic Advisors.

Where are all these good new jobs coming from? From new businesses or from small- to medium-sized companies that are being transformed into giants — firms like Amgen, Compaq Computers, Federal Express, Oracle and Staples, none of which existed 20 years ago. Other companies, such as Circuit City Stores, MCI and Nucor, were small niche players then, whose top management teams have since transformed them into thriving, vibrant concerns. And these are just the publicly traded companies. Countless privately held companies are creating millions of jobs as well.

Moreover, the types of jobs available have changed. The 30 biggest occupations now employ a smaller proportion of the workforce. Job growth is coming from high-paying occupations that did not even exist 30 years ago such as computer scientists and programmers, cellular phone designers, precision production supervisors and so forth. According to research conducted by Steven J. Davis of the University of Chicago and published in *Job Creation and Destruction*, 1 in 10 U.S. manufacturing jobs disappears over a typical 12-month period and does not open up again at the same location within the following 2 years. Other jobs, however, are being generated at the same time at a ratio of roughly one job created for every job lost. While this certainly creates some regional economic challenges (eroding tax bases, school closings, etc.), it is part of the dynamic of a successful economy.

Job creation and job destruction are intertwined, as Joseph Schumpeter observed more than 50 years ago. The essential feature of the capitalist system, he wrote, was "the gale of creative destruction," through which society adapts to changing technologies and consumer tastes and raises its living standards. For example, as recently as 75 years ago, the United States had 10 million registered passenger cars and 20.5 million horses, according to Census

Bureau data. Had the CEOs of that era been criticized or foolishly coerced into guaranteeing those jobs, the United States would still be stuck in the horse-and-buggy era.

What we are witnessing here is nothing less than a profound transformation in the way things are. It has nothing to do with CEOs enriching themselves at the expense of their employees. Industries and companies that were traditionally counted on to provide lifetime employment have matured; in the manufacturing sector in particular, they have started to decline. To avoid extinction, maturing companies are rebuilding themselves from the inside out. Unlike the Japanese, U.S. CEOs are motivated to choose among the difficult alternatives they face. AT&T and the Baby Bells have shed 30 percent of their workforce, or 300,000 people, since their 1984 breakup. In the process, they have halved the cost of long distance calls, doubled calling volumes, commercialized wireless services and made the U.S. telecommunications system the lowest-cost and most reliable in the world. Yet when AT&T Chairman Robert E. Allen is awarded 750,000 stock options,[1] he becomes a dartboard for critics of high CEO pay. Did he cause this sea change? No. Did he respond to it? Yes. And who could argue rationally that America would be better off if the former Bell System had doubled its workforce to two million employees rather than reduced it by one-third? While boards need to be sensitive to the employee and public relations impacts of some of their decisions, the financial point is nevertheless quite clear.

Although the individual pain and financial devastation of downsizing is real for affected individuals, job growth has outpaced population

---

1 Mr. Allen's options, granted at the money, have "economic" value but no intrinsic, or spendable, value, like a salary or bonus. They only will become valuable if AT&T's stock price rises over the next few years.

growth throughout the century and in recent times. At the macro-economic level, U.S. unemployment is low by the standards of the past 20 years and much lower than all of the country's major economic partners (Canada, the United Kingdom, Italy, Germany, France) except Japan — and Japan has its own economic problems.

Downsizing has become a fact of life, and, like it or not, it will probably stay that way. *Business Week* reports that in manufacturing industries, employment was down by 140,000 jobs from 1995 to 1996 as companies continued to cut costs. According to *Business Week*, there are still "large pockets of worry" in the service sector, where deregulation of the communications, utilities, banking and insurance industries has led to large-scale job cuts. But the proper response to this sea change is not to vilify those at the top. They did not cause the problem. In fact, in being paid to solve the problem, they have created companies more likely to survive global change and competition than ever before. The more proba-ble root of the problem is inadequate education and training to qualify for the jobs the new economy is creating. The solution to this problem — becoming more employable — lies outside the scope of this book. Nonetheless, it is important to remember that *efficiency* is always purchased at the expense of stability.

Fortunately, the economy has added approximately 11 million new jobs since the recession ended in early 1991, according to the Labor Department. And Americans who have lost jobs in the past several years have found new ones more easily and in larger numbers than in the early 1990s. Nor are the majority of these new positions just part-time "McJobs." The Bureau of Labor Statistics reports that over 60 percent of this country's displaced workers are getting full-time jobs, more than half of which are at equal or higher levels of pay than their previous positions.

While we should all be compassionate and responsive to displaced employees, the primary responsibility of top management is to create a climate in which companies can flourish. Insofar as CEOs and their senior executives have created the world's strongest, most resilient and most competitive economy, they have largely benefited American workers in the form of economically sound, not government-mandated, job security.

STRONGER RETIREMENT SECURITY

The second major advantage of CEO pay for performance is the increased value of employees' pension plan assets. Because pay is linked to stock price, CEOs are motivated to drive up stock prices through any strategic means. As the price rises, so does the security of pensions and other funds that workers have set aside for retirement.

Through company retirement plans and personal stock holdings, private households own roughly 80 percent of the outstanding shares of *Fortune 500* companies, according to CDA Equity Intelligence. In mutual funds alone, individual shareholders have invested more than $3 trillion, about three times the amount at the beginning of the decade, says the Investment Company Institute, a trade association in Washington, D.C.; approximately half that money is in stocks.

The long bull market has swollen many pension plan assets beyond what companies will have to pay to their workers in the future. Because these overfunded plans do not require current cash contributions (although they could be required in the future), companies have more cash and profits for expansion or other corporate expenditures. In fact, many sweetened early retirement packages offered during downsizings are paid for by overfunded pension plans.

A 1995 Watson Wyatt survey of 547 company pension plans found that the median ratio of pension assets to vested benefits was 129 percent and that 99 percent of these plans have more assets than needed to cover the value of benefits for current retirees. Another study of a large group of companies found that because of the bull market, 75 percent of large U.S. companies were "fully funded" in 1994, up from 60 percent in 1993. In total, these plans had $982 billion in assets to cover $853 billion in vested liabilities, for a coverage ratio of 116 percent in 1994. Given the spectacular U.S. stock market returns for 1995 and 1996, assets have increased by a very large amount. These statistics indicate that, as a general matter, American pensions are secure and becoming even more so.

Such overfunding also means companies can reduce or eliminate contributions for long periods of time, which increases their profit and, in turn, their stock price. "We haven't had to put a nickel in our fund for years," Ronald Boller, vice president of investments for Owens-Illinois, told *Business Week*. Overfunding also allows large corporations such as AT&T and GTE to allocate more pension assets to stocks than they typically would, as much as 70 percent rather than the typical 50 percent, according to *Pensions & Investments*. Such a large allocation means they can weather volatility and also reap greater gains from a strong stock market.

Employees with either defined contribution or defined benefit pension plans gain significant advantages when CEOs are motivated by their compensation packages to drive up stock prices. For example, the classic defined contribution plans, either 401(k) or 401(a) profit-sharing, frequently contain the employee's company stock (as an investment fund or as the company match) plus mutual funds that hold diversified portfolios of stocks and bonds.

Therefore, it is very much in the interest of employees that their own CEO, as well as the CEOs of the companies represented in their mutual funds, be highly motivated to drive up share value in both the short and long term.

Similarly, for a traditional defined benefit pension plan, it is in the interest of employees to have all CEOs motivated to drive up their companies' stock prices so that there are sufficient funds to cover future pension obligations. On average, defined benefit plans hold 43 percent of assets in stocks, according to the Employee Benefit Research Institute. However, the largest pension plans typically allocate at least 60 percent to stocks. These high-performing stockholdings increase the likelihood of a company meeting its pension liabilities and obligations. In reality, if the U.S. stock market had *halved* since 1990 (as Japan's did) instead of doubling, U.S. companies would have been forced to cut back on their pension formulas. It is well known that Japanese pension funds are facing a funding crisis in the near future.

All told, company pension plans reaped some $200 billion in capital gains in 1995 alone, according to *Business Week*. With stocks playing a critical role in funding both defined contribution and defined benefit pension plans, corporate performance can have a significant impact on the security as well as the size of pension benefits.

In summary, the very successful U.S. stock market, at least partly driven by executive pay programs, has increased the pension security of many Americans. In fact, in a survey of consumer finances reported in *The New York Times* in March 1997, the percentage of family assets in stock had risen to 40 percent in 1995 from 26 percent in 1989. This primarily results from the very large increase in share values caused by the bull market.

FUNDAMENTAL DISCONNECTS

Ironically, most investors do not stop to ask themselves, "Which do I want? A fatter pension or a return to the days of lifetime employment?" Instead, many choose to engage in one of today's most popular pastimes: the demonization of corporate America. In this regard, they are not unlike the news media. A *Newsweek* cover story, for example, labeled highly paid CEOs "corporate killers." *The New York Times* ran a seven-part series on downsizing, picturing workers on the brink of despair. But as we have shown here, executive teams are being paid to make their companies more competitive — and doing a good job of it. They are creating more and better jobs, along with greater employment and retirement security.

There is another fundamental disconnect as well, although it is not as obvious as the bad-news reports that the media provide about a strengthening economy. The organizations that pressured CEOs in the late 1980s to perform better — namely, public pension funds — are nowhere to be seen. The irony is that the public sector, in many ways immune to competitive accountability, has become the driving force of accountability in the private sector. Nevertheless, thanks to public pension funds, U.S. CEOs have proven that only a competitive economy can guarantee a robust labor market, deliver more value for consumers and more profits for investors, reward sustained performance and punish poor performance. This is a lesson slow to take root in Japan and Europe, as we discuss in the next chapter.

CHAPTER 3

The Role of Executive Pay in the Global Economic War: A Comparison of the United States, Japan and Europe

Japan's stock market is rolling like a snowball down Mount Fuji.

— *Time* magazine, February 3, 1997

Japan desperately needs to have stock options.

— *Tokyo Business*, January 1996

Most economists and other experts agree that the United States is winning the global economic race of the 1990s and is well positioned for the 21st century. Experts disagree, however, on the extent of the American lead, and they certainly disagree on the social costs associated with the country's economic approach. They also disagree on why and how the United States achieved its lead. But as we will see, by virtually every economic measure, the United

States is doing quite well, and the nation's executive pay programs have played an important role.

A myriad of factors affect a major country's economic performance: natural resources, geography, labor productivity, human capital, government intervention, education, history, defense spending, taxes, immigration, individual freedom, interest rates, currency exchange rates, stock markets, global trade and so forth. As far as we know, however, *employee compensation* is rarely cited as one of the factors to explain international differences in economic performance.[1] And *executive compensation* is either overlooked or only has been used as an explanatory factor to show why the United States was doing poorly. The stereotypical and most famous example of this arose during the 1992 Clinton-Bush presidential campaign, when the media attacked President Bush, the American auto industry and its executives. The substance of the attack was that the Japanese auto industry was significantly outperforming its American rivals, and Japanese executives were paid much lower salaries than their U.S. counterparts, as well as smaller incentives and no stock options. The putative theory was that the inherent "fairness" of the lower Japanese CEO pay levels motivated their hourly employees to higher levels of productivity. The big question was, "Should the United States pay as Japan does and thus be rewarded with Japanese industrial performance?"

Although this incident played a role in President Bush's electoral defeat, fortunately it had limited or no impact on American compensation practices. Even at the time, many U.S. industries, such as computers, software, technology and pharmaceuticals, were substantially outperforming Japanese ones. The U.S. auto

---

1 Martin Weitzman, author of *The Share Economy*, is a notable exception.

industry also quickly turned itself around and, as of early 1997, is being emulated by Japanese and other companies. And notably for our purposes, employee pay and executive pay played a role in this turnaround. All of the new compensation techniques — pay for performance, stock options, volatile bonuses (none in some years and very large sums in others), substituting bonus opportunities for salary and so forth — were tried by the U.S. auto and other industries with extremely favorable results.

This is not to say that executive pay is the only or even the most important factor in explaining international economic performance. Not at all. As we shall see, however, in conjunction with other economic attributes — particularly a highly dynamic labor market — volatile pay with large opportunities can make a significant difference. Should the United States consider Japanese- or European-style executive compensation programs? Even CEO pay critic Irwin Seltzer says the United States cannot "justify using economically moribund Japan or Germany, with its double-digit unemployment and sclerotic economy, as lodestars (in executive pay) for the United States." On the other hand, should the U.S. model be exported verbatim to Japan and other countries? Of course not! But just as the United States has learned from other countries, Japan and Europe should evaluate what the United States has to offer.

AN INTERNATIONAL ECONOMIC SCORECARD

Before describing the linkage between country performance and pay systems, let's examine how well the Western economies are doing relative to each other on economic and other job-related measures. We can start with an assessment of the morale of the famous "salaryman," the Japanese word for the classic corporate employee.

Salaryman represents the typical overworked Japanese manager, who has grown "alienated and burned out," according to Chicago-based International Survey Research. Only 44 percent of 8,600 Japanese respondents answered favorably recently when the survey firm asked, "Taking everything into account, how satisfied are you with your company as an employer?" Some 65 percent of American workers, in contrast, responded favorably.

This surprisingly downbeat reaction put Japan at the bottom of the morale heap in the industrialized world (see Figure 3-1). Workers in Britain, the United States, Germany, Mexico, Canada and Switzerland all responded more positively. In contrast, a mere third of Japanese workers judged their companies well managed, down from 45 percent in 1985. About 60 percent believe their work is not fairly evaluated, and only 37 percent think they are equitably paid.

Figure 3-1: Employee Job Satisfaction by Country

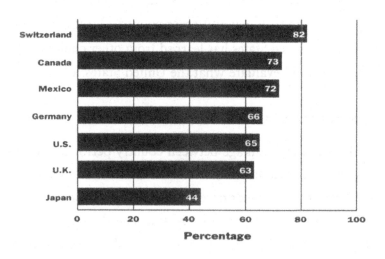

Source: International Survey Research, Chicago, Ill.

Worker morale points to many things that are not working right, or at least not as well as they used to, in Japan. At the beginning of 1997, the Nikkei had tumbled 20 percent from its 1996 high, extending a bear market that has eliminated $2 trillion worth of value from the Tokyo stock exchange's blue chips since their 1989 peak. With the Nikkei now down 50 percent from its record high, some experts predict it may fall an additional 25 percent or more. As *Business Week* summarized the situation, "The global economy is finally closing in on the country's protected, over-regulated domestic economy."

Half a world away, in Europe, one out of every nine workers is out of a job. Job creation in Europe over the last 25 years has been almost nonexistent. "If it weren't for a low birth rate," *Forbes* observed, "the rate of unemployment would probably be unbearable." With nearly a third more people than the United States, the nations of the European Union have created only 10 million new jobs since 1970, according to the magazine, compared to 46 million in the United States. European unemployment stands at 11 percent, compared to just over five percent in the United States for 1997. And U.S. stock market performance has been spectacular during most of the 1990s.

Figure 3-2 summarizes the global economic report card. While the European countries have strong stock markets, their underlying economies are not strong. Japan has a very weak stock market, reflecting poor corporate performance despite some other strong indicators, such as a low unemployment rate.[2] Overall, according to a 1996 International Institute for Management Development (IMD) study, the United States ranks first in global competitiveness,

---

2 The Japanese government measures unemployment very differently than the United States. Some experts say that Japan's actual rate is much closer to the official U.S. rate.

a rank consistent with other studies. The rank captures a large number of other economic factors including trade, savings, education, financial efficiency and the *flexibility of the labor market*. This ranking indicates a superior ability to increase national wealth.

Figure 3-2: A Global Economic Report Card

Country	Global Competitiveness Rank	Stock Market*		Economic**	
		% Change One Year	% of Record High	GDP 1996 Growth	Unemployment Rate
U.S.	1	+27	99	+3.4	5.4
Japan	4	-5	49	+3.2	3.3
U.K.	19	+16	99	+2.7	6.5
Canada	12	+25	99	+1.6	9.7
France	20	+29	99	+2.1	12.7
Germany	10	+31	99	+1.8	11.3

* *The Economist.*
**IMD Study.

Another indicator of the health of an economy is its cost of capital — the cost its companies face to raise investment capital from new stocks and bonds. The U.S. cost of capital in 1996 was at a multiyear low. This is due to high and rising stock prices and low real interest rates. As a result, new debt and stock issued each hit records in 1996 — $300 billion and $115 billion respectively, according to Securities Data Co. This is clearly a bullish signal for U.S. investment opportunities and the faith investors have in U.S. executives.

In contrast, it is interesting to note that despite Japan's collapsing stock market, its cost of capital remains even *lower* than the United States' (although it has risen since 1990). Nevertheless, investment and capital raised are negligible, since investors see little opportunity for returns in Japan's sluggish economy.

What is the specific impact of executive compensation on this report card? To arrive at that answer, let's first debunk the broader myth that Japan has a superior overall human resource or human capital model than the United States has, and that it would work very well in other countries, including the United States.

IS A NEW SYSTEM OF "HUMAN CAPITALISM" THE ANSWER?

Limping economies, high jobless rates, dissatisfied workers — what's going on in Japan and Europe? These were not the facts strutted by headline-seeking candidates during the 1996 Presidential election, when "income inequality" and high CEO pay multiples became campaign issues. Candidates claimed the United States was underperforming, which is clearly not the case, and they said U.S. executive pay was partly to blame.

Nor are these facts in support of other arguments that appear highly compelling at first glance. One argument in particular that typifies this genre[3] is worth examining in more detail. In his book *Human Capitalism: The Japanese Enterprise System as World Model*, economics professor Robert Ozaki at California State University contends that "human capitalism," his label for the fundamental model at the core of Japan's economic success, is "the most vital capital with which to create and increase the wealth of nations." According to Ozaki, human capitalism contains three elements:

- Management and workers "constitute an integrated group, assume primary sovereignty and behave as if they jointly own the firm."

- The humanistic firm "both competes and cooperates with other firms in the context of an organized market."

---

3 The other primary advocates of this "U.S. should import the Japanese model" argument are Lester C. Thurow, *Head to Head* and Derek Bok, *The Cost of Talent*.

■ Management and workers "substantially share decision making, the fruits of their work efforts and information."

Ozaki further argues correctly that human capitalism was "the foundation of Japan's postwar economic rebirth." But he argues incorrectly that the power of Japan's model *continues* and that "its principles are rational and universal and therefore transferable to other countries and cultures." This human capitalism is different from the generally recognized concept of human capital, although there is some overlap.

Obviously, two assumptions are at work here: one, that the Japanese economy continues to work well, and two, that the United States (or any other nation) would want to import a new philosophy of work, with its corresponding fundamental changes in compensation and reward structures.

Let's examine each assumption separately.

First, the Japanese economy did fare well — in fact, spectacularly — after the end of World War II, but it has not done as well in recent years. Recent indicators do not suggest it will again approach its former strength in the near term. Furthermore, the United States is clearly the world's largest and most productive economy — and by a considerable margin. According to *Business Week*'s Global 1000, U.S. companies now account for 46 percent of the $11.2 trillion value of the world's top 1000 corporations, compared with just 30 percent in 1988. Japanese companies, in comparison, account for only 23 percent of the Global 1000's value, reflecting a substantial recent decline. In addition, U.S. companies are worth 95 percent more than their Japanese counterparts.

Moreover, Japanese workers are only 53 percent as productive as Americans, while Germans — whose hourly wages average much higher than Americans' — are 90 percent as productive, according to a June 1996 report by the McKinsey Global Institute, the Washington research arm of McKinsey & Co. Measuring *wealth produced per capita*, another McKinsey Institute study found that the United States led France by 19 percent, West Germany by 25 percent, Britain by 39 percent and Japan by a mind-numbing 64 percent.

These statistics clearly indicate that there is an ebb and flow to this economic report card business. During the 1940–1960 era, the United States was the dominant economy; for the next 20 years, until the 1980s, Japan dominated with its superior economic growth. However, even during the heyday of Japan's productivity and growth, its absolute level of productivity was (and continues to be) well below U.S. levels. (Note the distinction between *productivity growth and improvement*, and productivity *levels*; both are important.) It appears that the United States is on top for the 1990s and well-positioned for the future.

For each of these successes — and setbacks — management paradigms have been developed to explain it all. While U.S. executive compensation is a catalyst for the current success, one other lesson is essential: Economies and managements must be flexible and must adapt to what will be successful. They must *not* "fall in love" with their own current techniques. Once again, as in so many aspects of life, the only certainty is uncertainty. Nevertheless, for the next decade or so, it appears as though the U.S. system will work extremely well.

How can this be, when American executives have been counseled so insistently to imitate the Japanese in everything from Total

Quality Management to "lean" manufacturing and now, executive compensation? While it is true that the Japanese have taught us much, many of their most storied accomplishments rest on the historical dominance of their manufacturing sector, which is only a fraction of their economy. Japanese productivity in the service sector, on the other hand, is very low — only half that of the United States. Yet the service sector, as in similarly industrialized nations, accounts for 60 to 70 percent of employment.

Much of Japan's historical success came from several other highly structured "business culture" factors unique to Japan (e.g., *keiretsu*, the special conglomerates; *kanban*, just-in-time inventory management; and *nenko/shushin koyo*, seniority pay and lifetime employment). While all but the latter and its special relationship to the Japanese team-based pay system are beyond the scope of this book, suffice it to say that once again the flows of global economic history have left this relatively rigid Japanese paradigm behind in the productivity race.

"Differences in productivity could not generally be attributed to differences in technology, capital availability, the marketplace, degree of unionization, economies of scale, production processes, capital intensity or differences in employee skill," comments Robert H. Waterman, Jr., co-author of *In Search of Excellence*, on the earlier McKinsey productivity study. In his book *What America Does Right: Learning from Companies That Put People First*, Waterman notes that the difference is what the McKinsey report called "division of labor," "management behavior" and government "policy and regulation."

What this means, Waterman concludes, is that across the industries studied, "America is better organized to earn superior returns on its investment in human capital. Labor is more mobile and flexible. Management attitudes are less rigid, partly because managers are less protected from competition and partly because they are more willing to experiment with new organizational forms. Government policy and regulation are less confining."

CONTRASTING U.S. AND JAPANESE EXECUTIVE PAY SYSTEMS: A MATTER OF ALIGNMENT

What role, if any, did U.S. executive compensation play in this high-stakes game of competitive advantage and rising productivity? Clearly, many factors help raise productivity and help a society's economy make transitions from one shifting period to the next. These include, in addition to Waterman's list, an entrepreneurial spirit and the desire to take risks. At the corporate executive level, these factors translate into the capability to make and implement the difficult decisions necessary to improve a company's productivity, including the sale of assets and layoff of employees. Social critics argue that CEOs take a cowardly approach to turnarounds by laying off employees. Management defenders argue that it takes courage to make this decision. Either way, it is inarguable that there is great *stigma* associated with layoffs, and it takes economic incentives, in the form of cash and stock option awards, to overcome the effect of that stigma. Without large incentives, a CEO would — and does indeed — walk away from the job.

But it takes more than just incentives. It takes an aligned social and cultural model. In the United States, a CEO who downsizes can be very confident that those affected employees will mostly likely be re-employed shortly at nearly comparable pay. He or she also knows, on the negative side, that the U.S. social safety net is not as strong as Europe's in terms of length of unemployment, health care benefits and so forth. Therefore, the laid-off employee is highly motivated to find a new job as quickly as possible. This is the core, the *sine qua non*, of the dynamic U.S. labor market, the engine of the nation's economic growth. *It is a great irony, with more than a germ of truth, that the most highly criticized aspect of the United States, by domestic and international observers — its low safety net — is also fuel for its engine.*

This system seems to work in the United States. The executive pay model is aligned with the labor market. In other countries with high safety nets, an aversion to layoffs and more modest executive pay, their systems — while also aligned — are not working for them.

IS THE JAPANESE MODEL EXPORTABLE?

Now for Ozaki's second argument — that Japan's "human capitalism" is transferable and that other countries should adopt it. In the United States, at least, it is the rare blue-collar worker or executive who wants to embrace the "ubiquitous signs of egalitarianism" scattered across Japan's business landscape — for example, the absence of separate dining rooms, bathrooms and parking spaces for executives; the wearing of identical uniforms for all employees; the modest differences in salary between blue- and white-collar employees. While executive perquisites are frowned upon in the United States as well, one need only look at a Microsoft or Wal-Mart, among dozens of other companies, to find employees that both understand and support the large earnings of their top, high-performing executives, because all employees share proportionately in the *largesse*. Indeed, a proud and prominent symbol of success in America, the land of the "rugged individualist," is the employee stock option, with the clear implication that a stock price climbing as high as possible is the key to prosperity and happiness, *despite* the outcome that the CEO will do well also.

The Japanese executive pay model would not work better in the United States than the current system. The Japanese model is characterized by relatively low executive pay (in absolute level as well as a multiple of worker pay) and low variation with or sensitivity to individual and even company performance. This approach was extremely successful for post-war Japan, although it has faltered since the 1992 recession. Some critics argue that this approach would have greater "equity," that is, be much *fairer*, if used in the United States, as well as be more *efficient*. The equity discussion is a philosophical and political one beyond the scope of this book, but it probably has some validity and needs to be addressed by boards and management.[4] The efficiency argument, however, goes to the core of our discussion. Would U.S. corporations be more profitable and competitive — that is, more efficient — if its CEOs and other executives were paid like their Japanese counterparts? In a word, no!

Some aspects of executive and all-employee compensation should be "synchronized." This is one aspect of Japan's compensation that the United States should and has absorbed. However, individual responsibility, pay volatility and pay for performance have served the United States well.

Before comparing the compensation *philosophies* of these very different cultures, take a look at data on the levels and types of pay in the two countries. *These data clearly will show that, on*

---

4 This is particularly true if there is validity to the argument that excessive CEO pay is creating social instability ("income inequality"), as argued by candidates in the 1996 presidential election.

average, U.S. CEOs are paid substantially more than Japanese chief executives. And the highest-paid U.S. CEOs, earning as much as $100 million to $200 million for outstanding shareholder returns, are paid even larger multiples than the highest-paid Japanese CEOs.

Steven Kaplan, an economist who researches executive pay issues, also evaluated the relative levels of U.S. and Japanese executive pay. His findings support our estimates that U.S. pay levels are two to three times higher than the Japanese levels.

The following table (Figure 3-3) presents some estimates in this regard. It is extremely important to point out that Japanese executive pay levels are *not* disclosed to the public under current Japanese securities laws covering publicly traded companies. This is, of course, not the case in the United States, where detailed annual disclosure is required (see Chapter 4). Even this disclosure issue is a distinguishing component of the complex socioeconomic nexus that sets these two countries apart. The United States, which conceivably has more to be embarrassed about because of its high pay, discloses everything; Japan, with nothing to hide, shows nothing. In fact, despite (or perhaps because of) extensive disclosure, U.S. executive pay levels have continued to rise. Intense information disclosure via the proxy in the United States has increased pay for performance, which may have in fact *increased* pay during the recent bull market. This is but another example of the very different roles and impacts of executive pay in the two countries.

These data would apply to the CEOs of complex, global public companies with revenues of $5 billion to $10 billion, one headquartered in Japan, the other in the United States. Higher

Figure 3-3: A Comparison of "Typical" Large Company CEO Compensation in the United States and Japan

Pay Component	U.S. CEO	Japanese CEO
Base Salary	$500,000 – $1 million	$500,000 – $700,000
Annual Bonus	50% – 150% of salary Very volatile	50% – 100% of salary* Not volatile
Stock Options	Very large Present value of 50% – 100%of salary Increasing over time	None
Other Long-Term Incentives	Most likely 25% – 50% of salary	None
Pension	Very generous but "unfunded"	Very generous Government mandated/ plus private (unfunded)
General Benefits	Yes	Yes
Housing Allowance	Rarely	Common Very lucrative
Other Perquisites	Some, but diminishing in popularity	Many; very important Golf club memberships are very valuable
Approximate Annual Total:	$3 – $5 million	$1 – $2 million (before additional tax benefits)

* Non-board member.

tax rates in Japan make CEOs' lucrative perquisites even more attractive, but not enough to close the gap.

There are those who argue that the global labor market for CEOs should rationalize the compensation of all CEOs, including those in the United States and Japan. By this they usually mean that *U.S. CEO pay levels should decline to the lower Japanese levels.* This would, in turn, supposedly create less resentment on the part of general employees, thereby enhancing their productivity. Obviously, this has not been the case, since the United States pays so much more and U.S. productivity is quite high. But does this mean that the global CEO labor market has failed? Not at all. Clearly, there are some Japanese CEOs who produce superior financial performance for their companies and who are paid a fraction of the comparable U.S. CEO's pay level. Why doesn't a U.S. board of directors hire one of these Japanese "bargains"? It has nothing to do with bias — it has to do with what is prudent. Is it worth $2 million extra to hire someone with the direct background to create potentially an extra $2 billion in shareholder value? The answer thus far is yes. Interestingly, the country that has provided the most non-U.S. CEOs for U.S. companies is the United Kingdom. That is also the country with pay practices most similar to those in the United States.

It is also important to note that Kaplan calculated that Japanese CEOs owned much less stock in their companies than U.S. CEOs in the mid-1980s. Since then, U.S. CEO ownership has increased dramatically.

Nevertheless, the executive pay system in Japan is entirely consistent with its general employee compensation system (and labor market, as discussed below). We believe that the U.S. executive pay system is also entirely consistent with the general employee compensation system (and labor market). Some critics argue that U.S. executives are more protected and insulated from pay and employment fluctuations than the typical U.S. employee because of their high salaries, generous severance packages, special bankruptcy protection and so on. These criticisms are overblown.

For the moment, all we need to assume is that the treatment of American executives relative to U.S. corporate general employees is analogous to Japanese executives and Japanese corporate general employees. (Certainly there are Japanese "salarymen," or middle managers, who complain about the huge golf club subsidies and paid apartments enjoyed by their CEOs.) This analogy allows us to compare the *overall* pay system in the United States with that of

Japan, without focusing on differences *within* U.S. or Japanese corporations. There are enough similarities within the individual countries to make this comparison valid. As will be seen, this comparison allows us to demonstrate that even under the remote possibility that the Japanese pay model could work in the United States, *it could take 25 to 50 or more years of cultural change,* which would have its own negative and unintended consequences. In fact, we, along with other observers, believe that Japan might benefit substantially from some U.S. techniques, particularly stock options and some pay variation based on individual performance.

Why is it that the Japanese pay system had been so successful in Japan and yet we believe it would not work in the United States? A pay system or model must be assessed within the context of other features of the labor market (e.g., training, job security, unemployment insurance). To take the most salient feature, would U.S. employees be willing to trade off job security for lower pay levels or smaller salary increases — in other words, receive theoretically smaller pay increases in exchange for job security (fewer layoffs)? While there are only sporadic examples of this tradeoff in the United States (e.g., union negotiations in the auto industry in the mid- to late 1980s and airline industry negotiations over the past 10 years), it is the exact model of most of the Japanese economy. Importantly, in the United States, these tradeoffs have occurred only in industries with general employee populations who are *well paid* relative to average U.S. pay levels. These negotiations were last-ditch efforts to save sick industries — sick in part because of high or "excessive" wages relative to global competition — and in general these efforts were successful. But would the entire U.S. economy benefit from these isolated examples? It's doubtful.

As Figure 3-4 shows, Japan and the U.S. have very *different* professional and managerial labor market structures and cultures, including very different compensation "anthropologies." It is astonishing that each of these economies could be as successful as they have been and yet have diametrically different compensation

Figure 3-4: A Comparison of U.S. and Japanese Corporate Labor Markets
Professional, Management and Executive Employees

Feature	U.S. Labor Market	Japanese Labor Market
I. Job Security/Safety Net/Structure		
Loyalty/trust between company and employee	Medium	High
Social safety net	Low	Medium
Freedom to change employers	High	Low
Risk of unemployment	High	Low
Length of unemployment	Low	High (Hidden unemployment)
Trust among employees for each other	Medium	High
Entry point into companies	All levels	Post-college, graduation only
Opportunities to recover from career setback	Many/frequent	Few; transferred to secondtier of economy
Stigma of being laid off	Low/medium	Very high
II. Compensation		
Wage flexibility	High	Low/medium
• Executive pay	Very high	Low/medium
Bonuses		
• Participation	Low/medium	Medium/high
• Variation with company performance	Medium/high	High
• Variation with individual performance	Medium/high	Low/none
Compensation variability	High	Low
• Pay for performance	High	Low
• Pay for tenure	Low	High
Overall pay multiple		
• Executive/all employee	Very high	Medium
• Trend	Rising	Stable

philosophies. Could it be that compensation policies and practices — particularly regarding management and executive incentives — have so little impact on individual, group and company performance? Or could it be that Japan's unique compensation philosophy — security- and team-based, with little individual variation, combined with *lifetime employment* — melds perfectly with that country's culture of mutual employee-employer trust? And could it be that the U.S. compensation philosophy — performance-based, combined with both *pay* and *employment* at risk — melds perfectly with a culture of individual responsibility for one's career? Which is it: No impact of compensation on corporate and national performance or high (though melded) impact on pay and culture?

Compensation systems clearly have a high melded impact. This latter belief is a direct challenge to those critics who say the U.S. labor market is too severe and "unfeeling," because it is so volatile. This volatility has economic benefit. Importing the Japanese model into the United States clearly would not work because the United States does not have the centuries-old history of cooperation and loyalty to organization, dating back to feudal and even *samurai* Japan. In fact, there is reason to believe that as the global economy becomes even more competitive for domestic corporations, the Japanese model could become less and less relevant, given its inherent inflexibility. Perhaps some balance between the two models could help Japan rise from the ashes of the 1992 recession, which appears to have been a watershed event in that country's postwar economic history.

CEO PAY AND SHAREHOLDER VALUE

KEY CHALLENGES FOR JAPAN

A key challenge in the Japanese compensation system is that employees do not participate in the *upside.* While this model worked well in the past, it does not appear to be working currently. "Microsoft millionaires" do not exist in Japan. While Japanese corporate employees have government- mandated pension plans, they do not receive stock options, nor can they participate in other equity-based programs, like many U.S. 401(k) plans. These incentives focus attention on stock prices and improve performance substantially. Many U.S. employees have an owner mentality, even those well below the executive level.

In Japan, however, employee stock options have just become legalized. Historically, strict regulations prohibited companies from buying their own stock. Nevertheless, for the time being, Japan's corporate employees are "hired help," toiling for fixed salaries with little in the way of stock incentive packages to convert them into "owners," other than the twice-yearly "bonus."[5] Even the bonus is not truly performance-based, because the average Japanese worker counts on bonus payments as a reliable source of income year after year. According to a Brookings Institution analysis, while bonuses usually constitute an average of more than 20 percent of the annual earnings of Japanese workers, their relative size is even greater for workers in larger firms. However, the report points out that while U.S. bonuses seem to be incentive payments, Japanese bonuses are not, because conditions for receiving them are rarely stated in employment contracts. "Whatever productivity effects bonuses may have in Japan," the report concludes, "it does not appear to be through their direct incentive effects." This is also directly supported by Watson Wyatt's consulting assignments with

---

5 Ironically, the Japanese word for "bonus" is *bonus,* borrowed from the English.

Japanese companies. It is, in other words, another piece of the Japanese labor market puzzle.

In contrast, U.S. bonuses, stock options, 401(k) plans and other profit-sharing plans do, indeed, raise corporate productivity — by as much as 10 percent, according to some studies — because giving workers a stake in a firm's success provides an incentive to work harder. Here again, however, individual incentives run afoul of Japanese cultural traditions. In a country where success almost always belongs to the group, rewarding individuals can generate friction inside the company. In addition, stock options do not work well with practices such as lifetime employment and seniority, which do not allow significant differences in compensation based on performance. Again, while the Japanese model — including no stock options — may have worked well in the past, it appears to have lost its behavioral power since 1990.

Japan had addressed the problem of group pay and incentives by institutionalizing "trust," a concept that some observers believe should be extended to other countries. Trust in this sense is defined as "the high degree of reciprocal moral obligation that the Japanese develop toward each other within the groups that they form spontaneously," as Francis Fukuyama, author of *Trust: The Social Virtues & the Creation of Prosperity*, defines it. "This sense of obligation," he continues, "is not based on kinship, as it is in China, nor does it arise out of legal contractual relationships. It is more like the moral obligation felt by members of a religious sect toward one another, where entry into the relationship is voluntary but exit is much less so."

Comforting in theory, this practice in reality means that there is no such thing as "equal pay for equal work" in Japan. In fact, it is "equal pay for different work" that holds sway. Indeed, Fukuyama concedes, "compensation is broadly based on seniority or other factors unrelated to the worker's performance, such as whether he has a large family to support. A worker... knows that he will not be fired except in cases of extreme misbehavior, and he also knows that his compensation will rise only as a result of getting older, and not in return for increased individual effort on his part. If the worker proves incompetent or unfit in some other way, the company, rather than firing him, will often find some part of the enterprise where he can be safely tucked away. From the standpoint of management, labor becomes a fixed cost that can be reduced only with great difficulty in times of economic downturn."

Normally in the United States and elsewhere, this kind of compensation system could invite what economists call "free riding," the practice whereby an individual shirks his duty but is still paid because the group as a whole performs well. That free riding does not largely exist in Japan is, indeed, a tribute to "the power of reciprocal obligation," as Fukuyama puts it. In return for stable, lifetime employment and protection of their long-term welfare, workers give the company their best effort. "In fact," the author notes, "the moral bonds that arise among employees at a company frequently take precedence over their actual families." These bonds between employees and managers are perhaps reflected most clearly in Japanese unions, which are organized along company, not industrial, lines. Thus, the Hitachi union represents all Hitachi workers, regardless of specialty. This means that Japanese unions hold interests in common with management in the overall growth and well-being of the company. In fact, the author points out, "Japanese unions often act as tools of management." Again, while this system worked well in the past, it does not appear viable in the new global economy.

It is very difficult to imagine such a situation working in Britain, France or Italy, with their histories of militant, ideologized trade unionism, or even in the United States. It is also difficult to imagine lifetime employment being implemented successfully in similarly low-trust societies.

How much optimism does this give us, then, about the importability of Japanese employment practices into the United States or the transferability of U.S. practices into Japan? Not much. Culture *is* destiny, to a large degree. Just as it would require decades of cultural change in America to make the Japanese pay model work, it would require a similar investment to make performance-based incentive pay work in Japan. The commitment to lifetime employment alone constrains the Japanese from downsizing and re-engineering to improve productivity.

Nevertheless, several major Japanese companies, including the extraordinarily large and successful Sony and Daiwa, have begun experimenting with stock options or their equivalent. In a recent article in *Tokyo Business*, author Masao Yamamoto describes how Japan needs stock options to be globally competitive with the United States. This article and the Sony program alone are major cultural and managerial breakthroughs. Since Japanese law has not historically allowed stock options *per se*, Sony had to go through what the author called "unwarranted maneuvering" to create the equivalent.[6] Obviously, the company thought it was worth the effort.

Why would Japan now need stock options or other incentives when it hasn't previously? Think of the stigma that is attached to U.S. CEOs regarding layoffs and other negative aspects of their

6 This law was changed in 1997.

jobs. The potential impact of layoffs on public relations and employee relations when layoff announcements are made — and the amount of public excoriation and humiliation — is enough to make every U.S. CEO think more than twice about cutting staff. Witness the well-documented situation with AT&T in late 1995, where CEO Robert Allen was pilloried in the press for announcing layoffs at the same time the company disclosed he had received a very large stock option grant. This negative publicity occurred despite the fact that the options were not "in the money" at the time of grant. But in the final analysis, opportunity for improved financial and stock market performance, combined with increased job security for the remaining employees, is too great and the stigma effect is overcome by the financial and incentive effects.

How much worse, therefore, is the dilemma faced by the Japanese CEO. Large companies have a 50-year commitment to job security and seniority (*shushin koyo/nenko*). Even if the CEO recognizes the need for layoffs, the stigma effect is huge — much larger even than in the United States. This is due to the large stigma attached to the *employee* who is laid off and his or her very inferior post-layoff job choices (unlike in the United States). In addition, Japanese CEOs were trained to grow businesses, not to manage costs through layoffs. This skill alone could require a full business generation to develop. Further, the job itself is not structured to make these difficult, strategic decisions, which require 180-degree turns in strategic direction. It is generally recognized that hard decisions need to be made by an *individual* in a *highly accountable* job; this is very different from the Japanese approach of consensus by committee.

Economist Lester Thurow, in his book *Head to Head: The Coming Economic Battle among Japan, Europe and America*, calls this distinction the difference between "individualistic values" and "communitarian values." As individualists, Americans believe in "consumer economics," as he puts it; the Japanese believe in "producer economics." As a result, shareholders are "a distant Number Three" on a list of three key stakeholders for Japanese firms; employees are Number One and customers are Number Two. As a result, "higher employee wages are a central goal of the firm in Japan," he writes. "Profits will be sacrificed to maintain either wages or employment. Dividend payouts to the shareholders are low." The time may have come to re-evaluate this model, as global economic pressures have made it no longer sustainable.

In addition to historical factors, there is very little *economic* incentive for the Japanese CEO and other top managers to make difficult decisions. Yes, if they turn the company around, they can keep their jobs. But clearly, this is not enough, and given the safety net for executives in Japan, it is not worth the stigma. *Merely dangling large economic incentives before Japanese executives in the midst of an otherwise aligned work culture model would not work.* It would probably create a form of work schizophrenia, where the executives would not really know what to do. A much better approach would be to raise the incentives while simultaneously making the labor market more dynamic and flexible. Shunsuke Takahashi, a Watson Wyatt senior consultant in Tokyo, strongly believes that Japan has begun to make significant progress on pay for performance. While they have much work to do, he believes the future looks brighter.

One final argument needs to be addressed in the context of comparing U.S. and Japanese executive pay: Would the U.S. stock market have risen as much — or even more — without all of these executive stock options diluting other shareholders' returns? In other words, is the positive incentive effect from options *greater* than the negative *dilution* effect? Or would huge pre-tax cash inflows from 401(k)s and "regular" pensions have driven up stock prices *without* "highly motivated" executives? While impossible to prove definitively, the case for stock options' incentive effect is strong. Here's what is likely happening in the United States:

- Executive stock options help to drive excellent financial performance;

- This financial performance increases stock prices;

- Rising stock prices make stocks more attractive for pension funds and for elective 401(k) allocations (and other mutual funds); and

- This further increases stock prices.

U.S. households are investing in the stock market, but the Japanese are not because they have no confidence in management and in their economy. They invest in bonds, which have extremely low returns.

OBSTACLES IN EUROPE

While the Japan-United States comparison is the most dramatic, cultural proscriptions also play a role in Europe. German workers, for example, place a premium on security and stability, preferring set salaries and bonuses to the ambiguity and risk of more lucrative incentive-based packages. And many German managers recoil at the prospect of giving evaluations on employee performance, let alone basing someone's salary on it. In Britain, simmering class tensions dating back hundreds of years still generate public scorn for wealth.

Government restrictions also play a big part in limiting executive pay. In Germany, high tax rates discourage large bonuses. Italy's pension reforms have severely restricted how much both the company and the employee can set aside each year for retirement. And in Britain, the government has historically limited tax breaks covering the exercise of certain executive stock options.

The historical nature of most European stock markets makes stock options an unpopular form of payment. Germany's bourse is traditionally very stable, and volatility is needed to make stock options valuable. With stocks often showing little price movement, it is unlikely that big gains can be made through stock options. German tax laws also require employees who receive stock bonuses to hold the stock for at least six years, reducing the incentive. Italy's stock market, on the other hand, is so enigmatic that executives would never consider a stock option plan; in addition, tax laws are unfavorable. Thus, executives prefer traditional pay packages with a base salary and standard bonus. It is a global tradition for executives to complain about how their stock market does not "understand" their company. It is clear that this is much less true in the United States.

As European companies become more global, however, many observers predict that executive pay will increase and become more volatile. A growing number of companies, mostly in the United Kingdom but also in Germany, are beginning to implement compensation packages with more variable pay, following the lead of the United States. Bonuses tied to company earnings, share price growth and other performance criteria are becoming more common. Britain has taken on many of the characteristics of the U.S. model, combining them with its own unique cultural attributes, with great economic success. The United Kingdom, while allowing significant upside opportunity in its executive pay, also has created ceilings, unlike the U.S. model. It's an interesting compromise that America and perhaps Japan should examine carefully.

Despite this international progress, Watson Wyatt's *Global 50 Remuneration Planning Report 1996/97* shows that the United States still tops the list in at-risk pay, at 29 percent of salary. Hong Kong, Canada, Australia and the United Kingdom round out the top five (see Figure 3-5). They all place at risk at least 23 percent of the total pay of a comparably ranked executive. While it is difficult to compare CEO pay around the world in an exact way, it is well known that the U.S. CEO is the most highly leveraged (i.e., has the most pay at risk).

THE "AMERICANIZATION" OF INTERNATIONAL EXECUTIVE COMPENSATION

In general, there is a greater impetus to import U.S. executive pay practices into Europe and Japan than the other way around. Watson Wyatt's consulting experience with U.S. subsidiaries of Japanese and European parent companies, as well as transnational corporate acquisitions, directly supports this trend.

First, with regard to the subsidiaries, until the 1990s the international parents were reluctant to pay fully competitive U.S. compensation levels to their U.S. executives, primarily because those levels were frequently higher than those in the parent company. The parents were particularly reluctant to replicate U.S. stock option programs that their employees could obtain at U.S.-based competitors. But after 1990, in a number of industries, especially in financial services and entertainment, parent companies provided U.S.-style programs in order to help ensure superior shareholder returns. European and Japanese acquirers of U.S. companies have realized the same conclusion. Finally, we have direct knowledge that U.S.-style executive pay for U.S. subsidiary employees has put pressure on the parent companies to modify their home-country plans. Presumably, excellent financial results will follow, as they have in the United States.

Figure 3-5: U.S. Tops World in At-Risk Pay
Median base salary, total cash and at-risk pay for 1996 by country (all amounts in $US)

| | Executive | | | Middle Manager | | |
	Base Salary	Total Cash	At-Risk Pay (rank/ percentage)	Base Salary	Total Cash	At-Risk Pay (percentage)
United States	275.0	385	1/29	95.0	109.3	13
Hong Kong	180.7	254.5	2/28	82.5	94.0	12
Canada	129.8	168.8	3/25	66.7	75.4	12
Australia	163.8	211.3	4/24	76.8	89.1	14
United Kingdom	250.5	324.1	5/23	79.5	90.8	12
Switzerland	210.8	269.9	6/22	119.5	137.1	13
Germany	245.9	308.9	7/20	133.9	152.3	12
Sweden	133.9	167.4	8/20	67.7	75.6	11
Czech Republic	61.9	76.2	9/19	21.0	24.6	15
Belgium	191.2	231.9	10/18	105.9	119.3	11
Italy	252.3	308.3	11/18	104.9	118.9	12
Poland	77.0	93.4	12/18	34.3	38.6	11
Mexico	260.8	319.5	13/18	75.0	85.2	12
South Africa	140.5	168.6	14/17	37.4	43.1	13
Philippines	132.5	159.0	15/17	27.8	29.3	5
Israel	101.6	121.5	16/16	56.0	62.3	11
Turkey	135.5	161.5	17/16	55.7	60.5	8
Singapore	143.8	169.7	18/15	62.5	70.2	11
Spain	137.7	159.5	19/14	73.2	83.9	13
France	208.7	238.9	20/13	113.1	125.6	10
New Zealand	112.0	124.6	21/10	54.4	58.7	7
Taiwan	N/A	N/A	N/A	87.1	107.2	19
India	N/A	N/A	N/A	7.4	8.9	17
Russia	N/A	N/A	N/A	39.4	45.9	14
Malaysia	N/A	N/A	N/A	37.7	44.0	14
Hungary	N/A	N/A	N/A	25.4	29.0	12
China	N/A	N/A	N/A	N/A	N/A	N/A

Note: Using exchange rates on July 1, 1996.

Source: Watson Wyatt Worldwide.

"Having watched successful American executives get rich," *Forbes* reported in April 1997, "talented European executives are no longer content to settle for high-taxed salaries and a chauffeur-driven limousine." German, Italian and even Swiss firms are turning to stock options as a way to motivate their senior managers. In fact, recent reports from Germany show Daimler-Benz and Deutsche Bank starting to grant employee stock options. The globalization of business is behind this trend. "As business becomes more international, so does the market for executive talent," the magazine observed. "Big international companies increasingly have to pay their best managers according to world scales."

Halfway across the globe, in Japan, Hiroyuki Tezuka goes so far as to suggest that the *very success of the Japanese economy is the source of its failure.* Writing in the *Sloan Management Review,* Tezuka, a senior representative of NKK America, Inc. (the major steel company), opines, "The sustainability of the key features of Japan's business system in the face of a five-year recession and the strong yen is in doubt." He further insists that it is "inevitable" that Japanese companies must abandon *keiretsu* linkages and *nenko*, seniority-based pay, replacing them with performance-based promotion and wage systems and contract-based employment.

As Soichiro Toyoda, chairman of the equivalent of the Japanese Chamber of Commerce, told *The New York Times* in January 1997, "If we take no action [to fix the economy] and let the problems linger on, the Japanese economy will be headed for catastrophe, and we will be left out of the world's prosperity in the 21st century." One of Japan's actions should be to re-evaluate its compensation philosophy. Why? Because the United States has the most competitive economy on earth, at least in part, we believe, because

American compensation practices are performance based. As aging European and Japanese economies are discovering, only a performance-based economy can guarantee a robust labor market and deliver more value for consumers and more profits and returns for investors.

Of course, performance-based drivers require a level of accountability unfamiliar and often uncomfortable for many European and Japanese CEOs and their boards of directors and management. The whole subject of corporate governance is being reviewed with growing urgency in England, France, Germany and Japan. As we shall see in the next chapter, the United States has made great progress in this regard as well.

CHAPTER 4

The Revolution in U.S. Corporate Governance and Its Impact on Executive Compensation

Addressing executive compensation should be a primary focus of every board, since it is at the very core of directors' shared obligation to monitor senior management performance.

— Report of the NACD Blue Ribbon
Commission on Executive Compensation:
Guidelines for Corporate Directors

If we don't (clean up executive compensation practices) we will see many varieties of...tax bills created by a willing Congress."

— Graef S. "Bud" Crystal, *The Wall Street Journal,*
July 30, 1984, commenting on golden parachutes

CORPORATE GOVERNANCE AND EXECUTIVE PAY

We started this book with a discussion of the reformation that has occurred in executive pay over the past decade. The trend in executive pay has been from *some* pay for performance to a *great deal* of pay for performance due to stock-based compensation. Critics argue that the U.S. corporate world has moved from very little pay for performance to an excessive reliance on stock appreciation. They further insist that stock appreciation may not, in fact, be linked to the underlying performance of the executives but to the overall bull market.

For example, the 1997 *Business Week* study of executive compensation argues that while shareholders can sleep soundly due to the pay/performance linkage, this "soothing lullaby" has some "sour notes." "The explosion of executive pay — propelled by huge option grants, easy performance provisos and a bull market — has created a windfall for all. Star CEOs are winning big, but so are many second stringers."

Having laid out these two positions, it becomes clear that while the causality may be subject to debate, the one thing they have in common is the strong linkage between the pay for top executives and the stock market performance of their company. *This explicit linkage was the result of a revolution in U.S. corporate governance, which caused not only changes in executive pay but other changes as well, including an increase in CEO firings.*

Just what is corporate governance and how does it relate to executive compensation?

According to Margaret Blair, author of *Ownership and Control*, corporate governance is more than "the structure and functioning of boards of directors or the rights and prerogatives of shareholders in boardroom decision making." Her definition also includes "the whole set of legal, cultural and institutional arrangements that determine what publicly traded corporations can do, who controls them, how control is exercised and how the risks and returns from the activities they undertake are allocated." In other words, corporate governance is the set of processes by which the total company is managed by the board for the sake of the shareholders and others. Clearly, executive compensation is an important part of that process.

Executive pay is arguably the primary mechanism by which the board can control and monitor top executives or at least signal to management what is important to the shareholders. And given the aggressive nature and the external source of the attacks and criticisms of U.S. corporations during the 1980s and 1990s, it is clear that a number of agencies and institutions believed that boards were negligent at worst or asleep at the switch at best in these roles. After all, it was not dissident board members or even solely corporate raiders — as part of a market for "corporate control" — who were the genesis of these changes, but a number of government or other agencies plus current large outside shareholders. As the quote from Bud Crystal indicates (on a different executive pay controversy), U.S. boards must continue to monitor themselves or the U.S. government could interfere. While great progress has been made, boards must continually evaluate the public relations impacts of their actions in addition to the pay/performance linkage.

A GENERATION AGO IN CORPORATE GOVERNANCE

To fully appreciate just how far U.S. executive compensation practices have evolved, one only has to look to the 1970s, a period that could be described as the golden era of executive pay excess. It was a time when:

- Selection of compensation committee members was the real key to CEO pay;

- Fixed pay ruled (salaries, bonuses, rich pensions and lavish perquisites);

- There were plentiful rewards but a paucity of risk;

- Control was a function of being an executive, not an owner; and

- Executive labor markets were plagued by various "imperfections," the most grievous being the lack of a *bona fide* arm's-length relationship between the buyers of executive services (the compensation committee) and the sellers of these services (the executives themselves).

This situation had arisen naturally. The United States had been the global economic superpower for three decades — since World War II — and had gotten a little complacent, a little "fat." Ownership of corporate America was truly diffuse. Investors subscribed to Modern Portfolio Theory, developed at the University of Chicago, under which they put their eggs into many baskets rather than just one or two. Further, then, as now, it was human nature to avoid risk, although today's governance process has corrected for this tendency by providing more reward as the *quid pro quo* for more risk.

Unfortunately (but not surprisingly) for the United States, the 1970s turned out to be a sad time of stagflation (inflation with no economic growth) and a prolonged bear market (really from 1969–81) — an unsurprising turn of events, actually, given the lack of incentives for corporate chieftains. The bottom line was that investments in U.S. equities simply did not provide a competitive return. Executives were not paid for creating value for their stockholders. Rather, they were rewarded for building empires — which translated into higher salaries (due to the overuse and misuse of compensation surveys) and large retirement benefits, none of which varied with performance.

Who needed to have the wealth of a king when you could live like one without it?

MORE RECENT CHANGES

The 1980s turned out to be a traumatic decade dedicated to correcting the excesses of the 1970s, primarily through radical organizational restructuring that allocated scarce resources to their highest and best use. This change, in turn, required a radical restructuring in the incentives provided to executives.

The first wave of restructuring was the mergers and acquisitions that led to the creation of the "golden parachute," i.e., special executive severance plans paid out at a "change in control" of the company. This was viewed by many as a "skid-greasing" device developed by investment bankers to open the doors to big advisory fees. It also was viewed as an extremely inappropriate reward for failure, although some studies did show parachutes actually *raised* sale prices. For example, Revlon's CEO received $30 million, considered an enormous amount in the early 1980s. Golden parachutes led to Congress's first real foray, in 1984, into the business of regulating executive pay.

The second wave of restructuring was the leveraged buyout (LBO) phenomenon, which turned the conventional wisdom about executive compensation on its head. Before LBOs, executives had no or low stock ownership, and share owners had diffuse holdings. No one was watching the store. Executives controlled the company even though they didn't own it. Then the KKRs (Kohlberg Kravis Roberts) of the world turned this situation upside down. After they bought the company, they required executives to own a big equity interest (reward with risk), leveraged annual incentives tied to interest coverage and lean fixed pay. In addition, the owner (a KKR, for example) had all or many of its eggs in one basket and watched that basket very closely. Directors had a large financial stake.

About this time other owners, particularly institutional investors such as CalPERS, the Wisconsin Retirement Board and TIAA-CREF, became restless, if not downright hostile. They had figured out they could no longer vote with their feet. A limited universe of equities made it impractical to unload a large percentage of a company's shares without negative reaction from the rest of the market. The only viable option, then, was to spur executives to improve performance. Of course, executives resisted fiercely. In 1982, for instance, General Motors' management would not return CalPERS telephone calls. (By 1992, the board of directors had asserted itself and would talk to CalPERS whenever CalPERS wanted.)

THE GOVERNMENT INTERVENES

Governmental and other agencies also figured out that something had to be done or the United States would slowly drift into economic oblivion. They all used their quasi-legislative or rule-making powers to try to influence corporate behavior. Three agencies in particular led the charge:

- The U.S. Securities and Exchange Commission (SEC), for legal issues relating to proxy reporting and disclosure regarding executive pay;

- The Financial Accounting Standards Board (FASB), an authority on the accounting rules covering corporations, specifically stock options in this case; and

- The U.S. Internal Revenue Service (IRS) for tax deductibility of compensation expenses.

The SEC Response

The SEC adopted sweeping changes in what and how public companies had to report to shareholders about executive pay via proxy statements. The SEC requirement was founded on the "sunshine" principle rather than regulation *per se*. Companies were directed simply to tell shareholders, in very clear terms and tables, how and why executives were paid what they were paid. Major changes to the proxy included:

- More summary tables, including three years' worth of pay information for the top five executives;

- A report *signed by compensation committee members* that summarized the policies on pay for executive officers, the relationship between pay and company performance, and the specific rationale for the CEO's pay; and

- Perhaps most importantly, a user-friendly graph showing the company's five-year total return to shareholders versus a broad market index and an industry peer group.

The overall impact of these SEC regulations has been very positive on the executive pay process. It certainly increased the amount of stock-based compensation since it looked so pro-shareholder in the proxy. Compensation committee members now take their job as agents for shareholders much more seriously than before.

The FASB Response

The accountants, innocently enough, also got into the swing of things regarding the accounting treatment of stock options and other stock-based forms of compensation.

A long-standing Generally Accepted Accounting Principle did not charge earnings associated with stock option awards; instead, only minor dilution occurred. A FASB technical review began innocently enough in 1984. It was basically an intellectual question about whether there should be a charge to earnings for options. If companies gave them to employees, there must be a value; if there is a value, there must be a cost, or so went the basic logic. Also of question was that other arrangements providing the same economic benefit to employees (e.g., SARs) resulted in dramatically different accounting charges.

However, after more than a decade of deliberations, the debate became political. Opponents of changing the rule — the Business Roundtable and high-technology companies, for example — questioned whether FASB's funding as a separate agency should continue. They "ganged up" on FASB, which received a great deal of support from the SEC (FASB's ultimate overseer). They also pressured politicians, although certainly not any from California, home of the high-tech firms that would have been hardest hit by the imposition of a charge to earnings for options.

The political issue resulted from two issues: one, that "fat cat" CEOs were getting rich without any expense or accountability; and two, it appeared unfair that stock options created a corporate tax deduction without creating an accounting expense.

After exhaustive deliberations and teeth-gnashing, FASB decided to let companies choose to continue to use the *no-charge* method but required that a footnote be added to the annual report.[1] This footnote had to show the effect of options on earnings, assuming that there was some cost associated with options (based on the Black-Scholes, binomial or other valid option pricing methodology). (See Appendix B for a discussion of the Black-Scholes option pricing model.)

The overall impact of the FASB ruling has also been positive. It has heightened the awareness of executives, directors and presumably investors to the real economic value of options.

TAX LAW CHANGES

During the Bush and Clinton administrations, several tax law changes have been made that affect executive pay:

- **$1 million cap Internal Revenue Code [Section 162(m)]** — Limits to $1 million the amount of compensation that can be deducted by a public company for any of its five highest paid executive officers unless the compensation paid to the executive(s) is "performance-based."

- **Rate hikes** — Ordinary income tax rates were increased to a maximum marginal rate of 39.6 percent.

---

1 Companies are "allowed" to take the full expense for stock options in their financial statements. Virtually no companies chose this method.

- **Qualified retirement plan limits** — Various limits governing tax-qualified retirement plans were reduced by President Clinton, including a reduction to $150,000 as the maximum compensation amount that could be considered in determining qualified plan benefits.

The most significant of these changes is the $1 million cap issue. Most companies have figured out ways to ensure the tax deductibility of all compensation. Those organizations that have complied with the letter and spirit of the law have implemented performance-based annual and long-term incentive formulas that have been approved by shareholders. Others require deferral of otherwise nondeductible amounts, until those amounts would be deductible. This law also strongly encouraged that compensation committee members be "independent" of relationships with the company in order to encourage arms-length negotiations over pay with the CEO.

Similar to other changes affecting corporate governance, these tax laws — particularly those regarding the $1 million cap — have had a salutary effect on increasing the relationship between pay and performance.

The Board Response

In addition to these governmental regulations, boards of directors have taken steps to ensure that their compensation committees truly are a *bona fide* arm's-length buyer of executive services. They have:

- Revised and expanded "charters" of responsibility;

- Appointed more independent directors to the compensation committees;

- Increased access to objective, outside experts on compensation matters; and

- Received additional and more useful competitive compensation information.

All in all, the impact of changes over the past 15 years has had a positive impact on Corporate America by increasing the resolve of boards and by driving management toward ever-increasing amounts of equity-based compensation.

On an international basis, Canada and the United Kingdom have been moving towards a U.S. corporate governance model regarding executive pay, flavored with their own unique political models. Canada has significantly improved its pay reporting disclosure. The United Kingdom has implemented the recommendations of two task forces — Cadbury and Greenbury — which developed strong policies on executive pay. These covered share authorizations, stock option grant sizes and related matters.

CORPORATE GOVERNANCE, SHAREHOLDER VOTES AND SHARE DILUTION

The most direct manner in which any governance process, including corporate governance, manifests its effectiveness is via its voting or electoral process. Apart from selling shares, voting on management proposals is the most direct indication of shareholder approval or disapproval.

Shareholders vote, typically via proxy, to elect board members and to approve management proposals on numerous topics — mergers, environmental plans, auditors and so forth, *as well as stock-based incentive plans*. Shareholders are given a description of the stock plan and then asked to authorize a number of shares (also expressed as a percentage of outstanding shares). Over the past decades, essentially 100 percent of stock requests have been approved. Now, however, for the first time shareholders are starting to bridle at these requests, despite their profoundly positive impact on shareholder value creation.

HAS DILUTION HIT THE SATURATION POINT?

Virtually all of the governance reforms discussed above have pushed U.S. corporations towards greater stock compensation for executives. These efforts have been successful in creating huge increases in employee stock ownership, including stock options. These increases in ownership have themselves been extraordinarily successful in helping to create the great U.S. bull market of the 1990s. *But are we nearing the saturation point?*

This question is important because the cumulative percentage of shares reserved for these programs is approaching a potential of 15 to 20 percent of the total shares of their employing companies. Virtually all of these programs provide stock to employees at terms favorable to public shareholders. While there are good reasons for these favorable terms, the size of the accumulation is nevertheless worth careful examination.

It is time to evaluate carefully the benefits to shareholders of all of these employee shares versus the cost.

The "incentive effect." To motivate employees to act in the short- and long-run interests of the shareholders, it is necessary to link their economic interests to those of the shareholders. This has worked very well in the United States but is nonexistent in Japan and arguably accounts for that country's economic shortcomings. Basically, the incentive effect says that by giving away shares or selling them at reduced prices, shareholders are prepared to live with a smaller percentage of the total pie. They do this because they believe that the pie — including their slice — will be larger in total because the employees will work harder, smarter and differently since they share in the pie.

The "dilution effect." The dilution effect is the amount by which the total number of shares could potentially increase due to employee stock plans. It is the employees' claim on the percentage of the total shares outstanding. (Note: It is related to but different from earnings dilution, which has additional components and accounting issues but is also influenced by employee claims.) Without an incentive effect, it would be illogical for shareholders to give away their shares, which are their property. Shareholders must be convinced that they are receiving a benefit in exchange for this dilution.

Economists know that when you have two countervailing effects from the same "cause," it is an *"empirical"* question as to which effect will dominate. In other words, does increasing the number of employee shares increase or decrease shareholder value (after subtracting payments to the employees)?

The following chart (Figure 4-1) illustrates the issues. While this is a hypothetical chart, the numbers are based on Watson Wyatt's experience.

At very *high* employee shares — say, clearly above 50 percent — there is *very little net gain* to shareholders, since employees are taking the lion's share of the value created. At very *low* employee

Figure 4-1: Incentive Effect vs. Dilution Effect

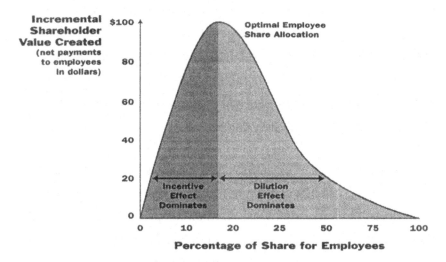

shares — say, below five percent — there is *also very little gain,* since employees are not motivated to improve the company's performance. There is some ideal level — maybe between 15 and 20 percent — where the incentive and dilution effects are optimized and there is a maximum benefit to both employees and shareholders.

Shareholders literally do control this balance between the two effects. Under securities law and stock exchange rules, shareholders must approve the allocations of shares authorized for employee stock plans. It is very unusual for shareholders to vote down a board- and management-approved request for shares. However, as the following table shows, institutional investors are setting up explicit policies for voting on share requests.

Survey of Institutional Investors Dilution Voting Policies

	Percentage of Institutional Investors
A. When Requesting Company Already Has 10% or More Dilution	
Vote of "No" is Required	30%
May Affect Vote	67%
Not a Factor	4%
B. When Requesting Company Already Has 5% or Less Dilution	
Vote of "No" is Required	4%
May Affect Vote	30%
Not a Factor	67%

Source: Investor Responsibility Research Center, "Potential Dilution from Stock Plans at S&P 500 Companies," 1996.

There are several reasons why share requests are rarely rejected, but two in particular stand out:

- Share ownership is quite dispersed; and

- Shareholders very broadly have a high level of confidence in their boards and their management.

However, as dilution gets larger, as shares become concentrated in institutional shareholder accounts and as more shareholders become "activists," it is clear that management must become much more careful, reasoned and reasonable in its requests. For example, if the share request includes a stock option plan for a large number of employees or all employees, shareholders will look more favorably than if it is an option request for the top 50 or so executives. This is another example of synchronizing executive and all-employee compensation programs, and it is viewed favorably by the employees and by outside shareholders.

MEASURING DILUTION: "OVERHANG"

Potential share dilution from stock-based plans is called "overhang" because it is the number of shares that hangs over the head of current real shareholders. Overhang includes options already granted plus options remaining to be granted (plus shares from other employee plans) and is calculated as a percentage of shares outstanding. The following example calculates overhang:

Current Outstanding Shares	100,000,000
Overhang: Options Granted/Remaining to be Granted (10% of current outstanding)	10,000,000
Total Potential Shares Outstanding	110,000,000
Overhang as Percentage of Total Potential Shares Outstanding)	9.91%

Overhang is calculated as either the 10 percent or 9.1 percent, depending upon the denominator.

As a practical matter, actual ultimate dilution is never as much as 9.1 percent. This would require that all options be converted to shares. First, employees leave the company before exercising their options. Second, many U.S. companies are making open-market purchases of shares to manage their share dilution. During the life of the option (before exercise), the company is not required to count the full 10 million options towards shares outstanding for the purpose of calculating earnings per share. Under historical and newly proposed U.S. accounting rules, only a fraction of the 10 million shares is counted. That fraction is based on the amount by which the options are in the money. This is called the "Treasury Stock Method."[2] Under the scenario shown in the footnote, prior to exercise only 3.3 million shares would be added

2 Example: 10,000,000 options at $20 exercise price

Current stock price = $30

$$\frac{\$30-20}{\$30} = \frac{1}{3} \times 10,000,000 = 3,333,333 \text{ shares}$$

to the 100 million, with the assumption that the employees' $20 exercise proceeds would be used to buy back shares on the open market. At exercise, the *actual* number of new shares issued would be added to the 100 million.

HOW LARGE IS OVERHANG?

According to a 1996 Watson Wyatt study, overhang at major companies is around 11 percent of shares outstanding. Figure 4-2 shows overhang in a number of important industries. This 11 percent is quite high by historical levels; as recently as 1990, overhang was closer to 5 percent.

Figure 4-3 shows overhang in the high-technology sector. This sector, like financial services, uses stock-based compensation plans extensively. In these two industries, it is well recognized that stock has been enormously helpful in creating shareholder value. Even here, however, it appears that shareholders are becoming impatient with the scope of the dilution. Boards and management must be prudent in balancing the incentive and dilution effects.

Figure 4-2: Overhang in General Industry

Industry	Share Overhang as % of Total Outstanding
Durable Goods	12
Retail/Wholesale Trade	10
Services	12
Insurance	12
All Industries	11

Source: Watson Wyatt Worldwide, "Executive Pay in Perspective," 1996.

Figure 4-3: Overhang in the High-Technology Industry

	% of Shares Outstanding		
	Median	Low Company	High Company
Options Granted	15.5	6	27
Options Available	8.9	4	14
Total	24.4	10	41

21 Companies

Source: Watson Wyatt Worldwide, "Taking Stock of High-Tech: Stock Options in the High-Technology Industry," 1995.

IN CONCLUSION

Shareholders, particularly institutional investors, have become more involved in corporate governance matters in general and executive pay specifically. The pay for performance linkage, particularly stock options, is the strongest way for shareholders to signal to the executives what is important to them. The various agencies that have addressed this issue, in concert with the shareholders, have been very effective in strengthening this linkage. And U.S. corporations are better for it.

CHAPTER 5

Synchronized Pay: A Solution for Improving All-Employee Performance

I don't think working people...resent people who run companies making a lot of money. What they resent is any feeling that they are being treated unfairly.

— President Clinton,
in a *USA Today* interview

U.S. companies should adopt pay packages that link compensation to increases in employees' productivity.

— Stephen Roach, Chief Economist,
Morgan Stanley

Not even Charles Dickens could have imagined an employer capable of such generosity. In late 1996, the Taiwanese founders of Kingston Technology Corp. in Fountain Valley, California, the world's largest maker of computer memory products, announced a staggering new standard for corporate *largesse*: a bonus package totaling $100 Million. Each of the 523 employees received a bonus

averaging $75,000, for a total of $40 million. The remaining
$60 million was earmarked for education and other employee
programs. The package made good on a pledge to give employees
10 percent of the corporate profits, a promise the founders were
able to honor when they sold 80 percent of the company to
Softbank Corp. of Japan.

The news ignited passions across the United States. Thousands of
job-seekers overwhelmed the company's switchboard. Letters to
the editor poured in to newspapers coast to coast. "It's funny how
two businessmen from Taiwan taught all of us a lesson in what
is supposed to be the American way," wrote one reader to the
Los Angeles Times. Wrote another, "My guess is loyalty is alive
and well at Kingston Technology, not because it was bought in
the form of a Christmas bonus but because it was earned by two
gentlemen who knew the value of their employees." Opined a
columnist for the *San Diego Union-Tribune*: "[David Sun and
John Tu] have shown other corporate chieftains that it is possible
to run a highly profitable, highly successful business while sharing
the wealth with faithful workers." As for the founders themselves,
their explanation was simple and straightforward. They decided
workers should share in the profits because they were "the ones
working hard day in, day out."

This concept of sharing the wealth is drawing increasing attention
as corporations create more wealth than ever before. The U.S.
stock market doubled in value — to $6 trillion — between 1990
and 1996. During the same period, however, corporations
announced a record number of downsizings and worker pay grew
more slowly than during previous expansions. Rising corporate
profits, along with large compensation packages for top corporate

executives, have fueled resentment among working people and perpetuated the notion that top management is compensated at the expense of workers.

Although we have shown that CEO pay by and large reflects performance, we do not believe that boards of directors should pay their top managers completely differently from the remainder of their employees. The long-term result is a demoralized and less productive workforce. Most aspects of Japan's compensation philosophy have not been absorbed into the United States. However, the concept of synchronization, which could be considered a Japanese human resource concept, has been used by a number of U.S. companies with great success.

SYNCHRONIZED PAY: A HUMAN CAPITAL APPROACH

This approach, called *synchronized* pay, makes workers' motivation consistent with that of managers and investors so that everyone shares the pain and the gain. Types of compensation are the same or similar, with payout levels clearly larger at the top to adjust for greater risk. Synchronized pay develops a consistency in compensation programs and payouts between executives and all employee groups. The most powerful example is a broad-based stock option program, which aligns the corporate culture to focus on improving shareholder value. BankAmerica's stock rose two points on the day it announced it would offer stock options to 92 percent of the bank's employees. Intel Corporation announced a similar plan in early 1997. The best way to make synchronized pay work is to have broad participation in cash incentives and stock options, reduce executive perquisites and benefits and make performance measures identical, if possible.

Jerry McAdams, Watson Wyatt's National Practice Leader for Reward and Recognition Systems, puts it this way in his book, *The Reward Plan Advantage*: "Companies are finally discovering that their employees are not just a cost of doing business, but potentially their most valuable asset. Turning this 'new' asset into a competitive advantage — especially in today's team-based environment — requires a new strategic business tool: a reward plan that can take the lead in shaping corporate culture, set the tone and focus of a change process, and support and improve upon *any* company objective."

Synchronized pay responds to the need to recognize human capital as well as investment capital. At a colloquium on "wealth creation and wealth sharing," convened by The Brookings Institution in 1995, senior fellow Margaret Blair argued that "employees are legitimate stakeholders in corporations for the same reason that stockholders are: both have invested resources in the success of the company." Blair's reasoning is that "the specialized investments made by employees in human capital are at risk in corporate activity in ways very similar to that in which equity capital is at risk." By this, she means that "the value of those investments ultimately depends on the ability of the enterprise to continue to generate an economic surplus." She recommends "maximizing the total wealth-creating potential of the firm, not just maximizing the value of the stake held by shareholders."

This is accomplished via investments in human capital made jointly by the company and the employee. The concept of human capital was developed by Nobel laureate economist Gary Becker in his book *Human Capital.* He applied the concepts of corporate finance and physical capital to the human resource. Focusing primarily on training, he determined that there were two types — general and firm-specific. Both general and firm-specific training cause the pay of the employee to rise. General training is valuable to *all* companies; firm-specific training has value only to the current employer. This difference in value influences who pays for — "invests in" — the training. This analysis is highly relevant to the current U.S. economy, where layoffs are common.

Basically, general training covers general skills that all firms would want — running a machine, accounting, sales, etc. Because these skills are not unique to the current employer, the employer will not pay the employee to obtain that skill. This helps explain why wages and salaries are lower when one enters a company and rise as one learns more general skills. The employee "pays" to obtain these skills in the form of lower wages. Experts estimate that general skills account for 70 percent of pay.

Firm-specific skills are by definition only valuable to the current employer. Unique systems or approaches to all areas — production, marketing, finance, etc. — fall into this category, as does an understanding of the company's culture or "politics." These specific types of skills range from knowing where the cafeteria is to knowing which senior executive has real power — all productivity-improving skills at *this particular company*. The company "pays" for this training received by the employee while he or she makes this investment. This represents the other 30 percent of wages. *If the employee is laid off, other companies will not pay this 30 percent.* This explains why some employees have lower pay after a layoff. However, the company loses the 30 percent also; it is as if it shut down 30 percent of its machinery.

It is essential, therefore, that companies go to great lengths not to lose this 30 percent from firm-specific training. It is the *economic* reason why layoffs tend to be the strategy of last resort. For sound economic reasons, employees must be treated as *owners*, just like shareholders. Both groups face risks from a poorly run company.

MAKING THE TRANSITION

Fortunately, corporations have made a great deal of progress in this area of synchronized pay and valuing their human capital since the early 1980s. The typical compensation system then featured very different executive and all-employee programs. The executive program had relatively high salaries and narrow salary grades. Executives received annual incentives and stock options, and they typically had a Supplemental Executive Retirement Plan (SERP).[1] All other employees, however, had average salaries and narrow grades. Benefits were competitive, but they did not usually include stock options, stock purchases, annual incentives or special benefits.

Today's compensation programs, in comparison, show significant progress toward synchronization. The typical executive program still has average salaries, but now it may have career bands as well. These "broadbands" reduce the number of salary grades but increase the amount of money available in each grade. They represent major opportunities for creating synchronized programs because they develop an atmosphere of fairness. Individuals can be rewarded for their own competence level instead of having their pay based on a narrower job classification. Executives today also receive larger annual incentive payments, frequently paid in stock,

---

1 A SERP is a pension plan for top managers; its features are typically more generous than those in all-employee plans.

and very large stock option grants. Stock incentives show a tremendous management commitment toward improving corporate performance.

The typical all-employee program today still features average salaries, as few companies can take the risk of high fixed costs, but they either have bands or are considering moving toward them. Many now provide annual incentives, certainly for their non-hourly workers, and many are considering expanding incentives to all employees. Financial measures for incentive plans are similar to those for top managers. Stock purchase plans are commonplace, particularly the opportunity to buy stock at a 15 percent discount. And stock options, formerly the province of only very senior managers, are now routinely available to all employees in start-up and high-technology companies and increasingly in other organizations as well.

KEY CHARACTERISTICS AND ARCHITECTURE

The one truly stellar example of progress, however, is the growing emphasis on pay for performance. Without a doubt, this is the most critical attribute of a synchronized culture, and it must be exemplified at the top. Since we have shown that most corporations do, indeed, pay their chief executive officers according to their performance, then a successful synchronized pay program should do the same. This means that the key characteristic should be consistency — consistent application of the same criteria for all compensation programs throughout the company. Not *foolish* consistency, as Ralph Waldo Emerson warned against — not identical programs but similar ones.

With consistency as the cornerstone, several areas deserve explicit consideration when establishing synchronized pay programs:

1) *Maintain three basic types of compensation programs for all employees: salary, annual incentives and long-term incentives, typically stock options.* Start with that model and move away from it only for good reason. Naturally, allow for greater opportunities for larger jobs.

2) *Performance measures should be identical, if possible, and the same for all employees from the top down.* Possible measures include total return to shareholders, earnings per share, net income, return on equity and economic value added. To ensure that your incentive plans will maximize motivation, you must also balance those financial measures, if possible by utilizing "line-of-sight" measures. However, line-of-sight measures — those which can be most directly impacted by employees, since they are "in sight" — require careful thought. Serious problems can develop if top managers are measured on a financial measure — for example, return on equity — and receive their full incentive, while the rest of the employees are appraised on line-of-sight measurements and fall short of the mark. When this occurs, a terrible morale problem erupts, resulting in a demoralized workforce. On the other hand, no line-of-sight measures are also a problem.

3) *Executive perquisites and benefits should be eliminated or reduced, if possible.* For example, executive medical benefits should be eliminated and replaced with salary. Otherwise, how can a CEO raise deductibles or premiums or emphasize HMOs when the proxy describes a special $50,000 fund for medical benefits?

4) *Performance management programs should cover all employees, including CEOs.* Boards of directors should establish special committees to review the CEO's performance every year. Probably fewer than 25 percent of companies do this now, and that is not enough. Performance appraisals for all employees, including those at the top, are essential for creating a synchronized performance-based culture.

Companies in the process of establishing a synchronized pay program can benefit from following a simple architecture, but it must be expressly tailored for their culture. First and foremost, they should develop a strong business case. Changing a compensation system, even one that is working poorly, holds the potential for heightening employee anxiety. Therefore, reasons for the change should be framed in strategic terms. If the company is facing tectonic shifts in its industry caused by deregulation, for instance, that is a good reason to begin aligning compensation measures and methods across the board. Make the business case compelling — a major strategic threat, the need to reposition to capture greater market share, etc. — so that employees understand how the business has changed the need to be paid differently. And make sure that the business case envisions that employees' paychecks will be different five years from now than they would have been — both in magnitude and in who receives how much — because that is the fundamental purpose of synchronized pay.

Another key architectural element is educating employees about the measures on which their compensation is based. Financial information should be communicated continuously in ways employees can best understand it. Finally, the program's impact and outcome should be reviewed regularly, with a view toward modifying the plan in years to come as different needs are determined.

EXAMPLES OF SUCCESSFUL PROGRAMS

Does synchronized pay work in the real world? Yes, indeed. Just look at the U.S. auto industry. In exchange for wage freezes and cuts, unions insisted on an incentive plan that guaranteed payments to unionized workers whenever top management received payments. Synchronizing the incentives put an end to special executive bonuses that were not replicated for union employees. It also caused tough decisions to be made that helped turn that industry around in the 1980s.

At one of Watson Wyatt's clients in the electric utility industry, annual line-of-sight incentives are helping them become more competitive. Many pharmaceutical, technology and consumer products companies, including Pfizer, Intel, Apple, Pepsi and Du Pont, have introduced stock option programs for all employees. Fast-food operations like Starbucks and Wendy's International credit their stock option program with reducing turnover dramatically among managers and counter help alike. In fact, 1996 data from Sanford C. Bernstein & Co. estimate that there are $600 billion worth of employee options in the United States.

How does synchronized pay work best? Two case studies provide good direction. Both involve start-up organizations spun off from much larger corporate parents. In both instances, these companies started with clean slates.

The first company is the financial services division of a non-financial *Fortune 100* corporation. The company intended to capture sizable market share quickly by relying on three principal strategies: differentiate based on customer service, leverage the parent company's strong balance sheet and capitalize on the parent's household brand name. The company organized around customer-focused process teams, rather than by departments, so that employees could serve different industries and different types of customers. Quite deliberately, the reward structure was completely consistent with the organizational design. Every single compensation program was tied to customer service. Job functions were grouped into broad salary grades, and salary was based on competencies. All-employee annual incentive plans were tied to customer service measures. Even long-term incentive plans used customer service as a measure. Executive incentives were tied to shareholder value and to winning the Malcolm Baldrige National Quality Award, which the company subsequently did. Since the division did not have stock available, this was a creative example of using cash compensation to create a synchronized culture.

Another example involves a major retailer that spun off some of its specialty subsidiaries and was therefore able to use stock as compensation. Three principal business strategies were implemented: strengthen a separate identity for the spinoffs, continue their high-growth trend and differentiate by controlling and creating an entrepreneurial culture. It was critical to build an ownership culture among all employees and to emphasize store performance. Therefore, the reward system linked every employee by two or more programs to some kind of stock-based compensation program, including a stock purchase plan at the executive level on a non-qualified basis and at the all-employee level on a qualified basis. Annual incentives were tied to store results. Salary increases were reduced, and the parent company's qualified pension plan was terminated, replaced by a qualified profit-sharing plan that paid out in company stock. The pay programs of all the spinoffs were highly synchronized, and the companies have been extremely successful since their initial public offerings.

STRATEGIC REWARDS

The common point in both these stories is that synchronized pay was used to treat employees fairly and honestly and motivate strong performance at the same time. These are the principal benefits of what we call "strategic rewards." As the name implies, these rewards are an integral part of a company's business plan, aligned with strategies that drive the business externally and internally.

Do strategic rewards deliver the desired results? In a 1996/1997 Watson Wyatt study of 698 companies employing over five million workers, companies that cited recent increases in their net operating income (NOI) reported stronger links between strategy and rewards (see Figure 5-1). Increasing NOI companies were twice as likely as those with decreasing NOI to say their reward programs were closely tied to their companies' strategies. Moreover, companies with rising NOI were much more likely to characterize their reward programs as sensitive to business performance.

Figure 5-1: Strategy, Business Performance and NOI

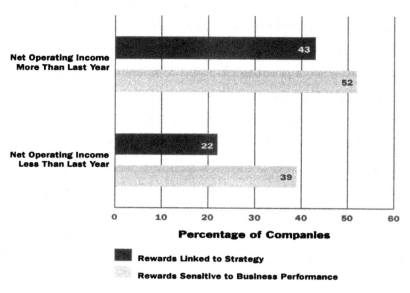

In other research measuring the effect of strategic rewards on total return to shareholders (TRS) over three years, Watson Wyatt saw similar correlations. Examining a broad array of specific compensation programs, TRS is highest when existing reward plans are linked to business strategy (see Figure 5-2), when existing reward plans encourage desired culture and behaviors (see Figure 5-3), when existing compensation strategy is clearly articulated (see Figure 5-4), when employees value the existing reward plan (see Figure 5-5) and when existing reward plans are measured on an ongoing basis (see Figure 5-6). TRS is also higher at companies that have implemented strategic rewards programs for hourly workers and professionals (see Figure 5-7).

Figure 5-2: Business Objectives
To what extent are your existing reward plans linked to your business strategy?

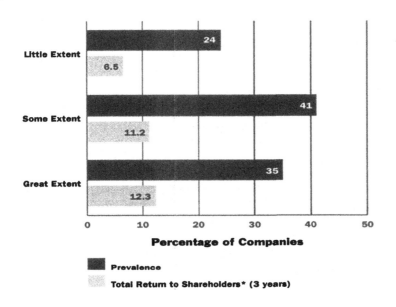

* 3 years for 228-company subset

Figure 5-3: Desired Culture
To what extent do your existing reward plans
encourage desired culture and behaviors?

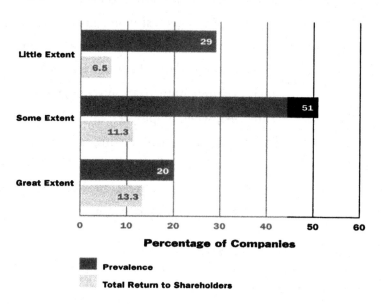

Figure 5-4: Awareness
To what extent is your existing compensation strategy
clearly articulated?

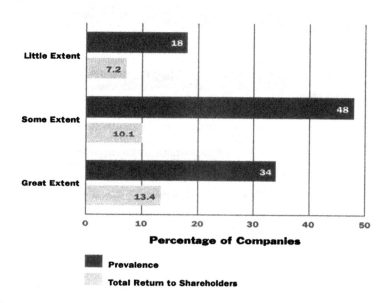

Figure 5-5: Value
To what extent do your employees value
your existing plan?

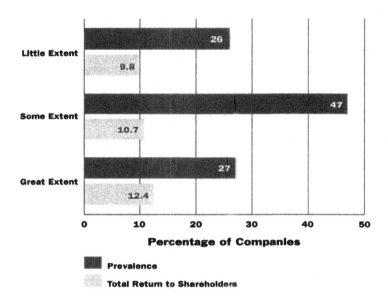

Figure 5-6: Measurement
To what extent are your existing reward plans
measured on an ongoing basis?

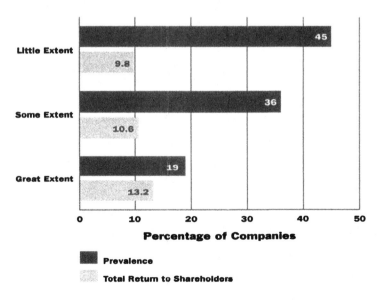

While these survey data cannot be used to conclusively attribute financial success to well-designed reward programs, they do reveal compelling correlations. At a time when the world of work has changed dramatically, companies need the added flexibility that synchronized pay and other strategic rewards programs deliver. They need every tool available to facilitate stronger alignment between corporate objectives and shareholder value. In the challenge to improve competitive performance, strategies for sharing the wealth deserve as much attention as strategies for creating it.

Figure 5-7: TRS and Strategic Rewards

	TRS of Companies			
	Hourly Workers		vs.	Professionals
Type of Plan	Yes*	No**	Yes	No
Annual Bonuses	16.4%	10.4%	13.5%	9.5%
Lump-sum Merit Increases	14.4	10.0	13.6	9.9
Group Incentives	13.4	10.2	12.6	10.0
Profit Sharing	13.3	10.0	13.2	10.1
Stock Options	19.2	10.7	13.3	10.3

* Have plan.
**Do not have plan.

CHAPTER 6

U.S. Executive Stock Ownership: A Source of Competitive Advantage

*"If the CEOs of America would follow suit,
I'd be back playing the piano."*

— Graef S. "Bud" Crystal, commenting on
Jerre Stead's all-stock compensation
package, in *The New York Times*

It may be the most daring pay package in all of corporate America. Upon leaving his position as CEO of AT&T's NCR subsidiary, Jerre L. Stead opted to receive no cash salary whatsoever when he signed on in August 1996 as CEO of Ingram Micro, Inc., a computer distributor in Santa Ana, California. Instead, he gained the right to purchase 3.6 million shares of Ingram Micro's stock — 400,000 when the company went public in the fall of 1996, 1.6 million in four installments beginning in April 1998 and the rest on a schedule tied to goals for the stock price and company earnings. In theory, according to *The New York Times*, he could own 2.8 percent of the company in five years. If he triples the stock price in that time, his stake will be worth over $100 million. If he falls short of the mark, he will have worked — literally — for nothing.

We have been discussing the powerful incentive of linking stock prices to executive pay. Obviously, stock options can be extremely successful in this regard. However, as discussed in *Value at the Top*, we recognized as early as 1992 that direct stock ownership (in addition to options) was essential to balance some of the excessive risk taking that could be encouraged by options alone. Stock purchase or acquisition plans are extremely helpful in achieving ownership targets that many companies set. As a result of these and other plans, the direct stock ownership of U.S. executives has increased substantially over the past decade.

Certainly there has been an order-of-magnitude increase in CEO stock ownership in large companies. Don't expect sizable numbers of chief executive officers to mimic Mr. Stead's compensation plan, but don't be surprised to see half of the top 1,000 companies in America requiring their senior executives to own a healthy share of the companies they manage. This would continue a trend that began picking up speed in the late 1980s. In Watson Wyatt's latest survey of executive pay, a growing proportion of companies require ownership, with two-thirds using the executive's base salary for the ownership multiple (see Figure 6-1).

Of course, the principal reason driving executive stock ownership is the desire by both the company and outside investors for senior managers to have a significant stake in the success of the business — to have their fortunes rise and fall with the value they create for shareholders.

Figure 6-1: Stock Ownership Guidelines

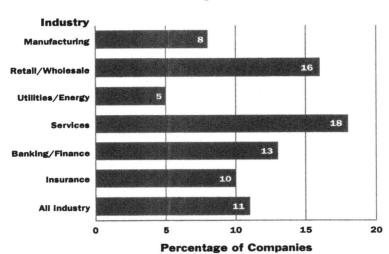

Industry

Percentage of Companies

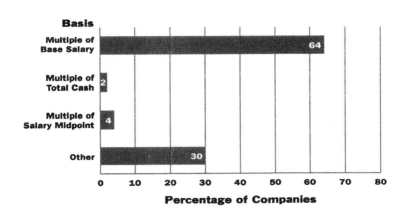

Basis

Percentage of Companies

Such ownership can be worth several percentage points in returns to shareholders. Watson Wyatt's 1996 survey shows that high levels of stock ownership are linked to high levels of financial performance (Figure 6-2). Companies with above-median stock ownership among CEOs ($45 million) had an average total return of 21 percent annually, while companies with below-median ownership ($4 million) posted an average annual return of 15 percent. All CEOs in Watson Wyatt's study own nearly $12 million worth of stock, excluding stock options.

Figure 6-2: Companies with High CEO Stock Ownership Perform Better than Low-Ownership Companies

CEO Stock Ownership*	Median Value of CEO's Stock ($ millions)	Median Multiple of Salary to Stock Value	Percent Annualized TRS**
High	45.0	78:1	21
Low	4.4	7:1	15
All	11.8	17:1	18

* High = Above the median; Low = Below the median

**Five-Year Total Return to Shareholders (TRS)
(TRS = Stock price appreciation + dividends ÷ beginning stock price)

Source: Watson Wyatt study of 398 large public companies with CEOs with more than five years of tenure as CEO.

Watson Wyatt's study is not alone in confirming that executive ownership creates meaningful gains in shareholder value. The Council of Institutional Investors, an association of public, corporate and Taft-Hartley pension funds, gathered a number of studies on the impact of executive and employee stock ownership. More than 90 percent of those that reached a conclusion showed that high levels of ownership improved performance.[1]

Bud Crystal, for example, has found that shareholder value increases in large capitalization companies as the CEO's shareholdings increase. Specifically, Mr. Crystal determines that over the nine years prior to July 1991, "for each additional $1,000 of shares a CEO holds, the company's shareholders might look forward to an added $23,000 increase in the aggregate value of their shareholdings." Another study, this one by Professors Sharon Oswald and John Jahera of Auburn University, further shows that all performance measures — rate of return on assets, rate of return on equity and

1 Performance is broadly expressed as stock price appreciation and increased financial performance, but other financial measures were used.

excess returns — are higher for those companies with the greatest degree of inside — i.e., executive — ownership.

Yet another study demonstrates that managerial ownership of stock is significantly related to above-market returns of 23.4 percent in successful takeovers. Professors Moon Song of San Diego State University and Ralph Walkling of Ohio State University point out that management's greater stake in equities increases their bargaining power, which managers can use to earn increased returns for their shareholders.

John Reed, Citicorp's CEO, represents one of the most dramatic examples of the successful impact of executive stock ownership on a company. In the late 1980s, when Citicorp was struggling to turn itself around from real estate and other problem loans, its stock was tumbling. Reed made a dramatic open-market purchase of a large number of shares, indicating his personal commitment to the stock and to the company. In the following years, he put in a number of creative compensation programs, many of which were designed to create ownership. He also led his team in a dramatic restructuring and refocusing of the company. All of these efforts worked. Citicorp is a top-performing bank and stock. And Reed owns more than one million shares as of 1997, with additional stock options worth well over $100 million. His vote of confidence paid off. Other large CEO shareholders — other than founders — are Michael Eisner of Disney and Robert Goizueta of Coca-Cola, who own $600 million and *$1 billion* of stock, respectively. These huge amounts represent their reward for increasing shareholder value by nearly $50 billion and $100 billion.

Requiring CEOs to purchase their companies' stock, in addition to receiving options, is the most effective way to ensure that CEOs take prudent, not unnecessary, risks to increase shareowner value. Stock purchase plans work for two reasons:

- First, executives holding solely stock options have only upside opportunities, compared to the shareholders they represent, who also face downside risks. This can result in more aggressive risk-taking by executives because they have nothing to lose.

- Second, options generally do not result in ownership, since most employees, including executives, sell the stock shortly after exercise.

Grants of restricted stock, as opposed to purchases, also have drawbacks, the primary one being the negative perception that boards of directors are "giving stock away." In addition, the CEO faces even less risk with restricted stock than with options. Unless the share price drops to zero, the executive will always have a gain. Nevertheless, both stock options and restricted stock can have their appropriate uses.

STOCK OWNERSHIP GUIDELINES

The key to developing the shareholder/executive linkage is to get the executives to do what the shareholders have done — purchase the stock. Ford Motor Co. instituted the practice in 1995, requiring 41 top executives to hold as much as five times their salary in stock. Companies with similar guidelines include American Express, Intel, BankAmerica, Bell Atlantic, J.P. Morgan and many others. Xerox makes compliance with its stock ownership guidelines a condition for participating in other incentive programs. According to *Barron's*, about 20 percent of U.S. companies with annual revenues greater than $1 billion now require executive stock ownership. Even company directors, responsible for representing shareholders' interests, are increasingly being paid in stock.

Under most guidelines, a company's senior executives are encouraged to own a certain multiple of their salaries in stock. While the multiple can be as high as 10, it typically ranges from five to seven, depending on the executive's seniority. For example, if the multiple is five and the salary is $200,000, the required amount of stock would be $1 million. Most guidelines further specify that executives amass the required shares of stock within three to five years from the time the guidelines are adopted. Most ownership guidelines have been implemented over the past three years, a bull market. It remains to be seen what the outcome will be if there is a market correction.

At companies like J.C. Penney, *Barron's* reports, the guidelines cover everyone from the company's CEO, who must hold shares equivalent to seven times his base salary, all the way down to store managers, who must own stock equal to 50 percent of their base salary. Such ownership guidelines must be tailored to the unique culture and history of the company. For example, a company with a long history of stock option grants and rising stock price performance might have higher guidelines than another company with poorer stock price performance. In either case, however, the guidelines themselves could help with future stock price increases.

Baxter International's program went so far as to arrange bank loans for 70 executives to buy company stock from treasury reserves, guaranteeing the loans if a manager went bankrupt. Purchases amounted to multiples of 6 to 10 times the executives' annual salary. Vernon Loucks, Baxter chairman, borrowed $9 million to purchase 350,000 Baxter shares, more than his net worth. As he told Barron's, "The point is that if the company fails, the bank will get everything I've got." So far, he is safe. Baxter stock has nearly doubled since the company underwent a radical restructuring in 1993.

EXECUTIVE STOCK PURCHASE PROGRAMS

Many companies face the problem of how to encourage management to achieve these desired ownership levels of company stock. As important as stock option programs are, they have not been successful in creating high levels of executive stock ownership. Approaches vary from motivating with the carrot to "requiring" with the stick. Companies have tried all types of plans to create ownership (see Figure 6-3 and Appendix A). These include, in addition to stock options, performance shares and grants of restricted stock. Each of these has its advantages and disadvantages. In addition, some companies have recognized that higher levels of ownership can be encouraged through a non-qualified stock purchase plan, what Watson Wyatt calls a Management Stock Purchase Plan (MSPP).

Figure 6-3: Types of Long-Term Incentive Vehicles (All Industries)

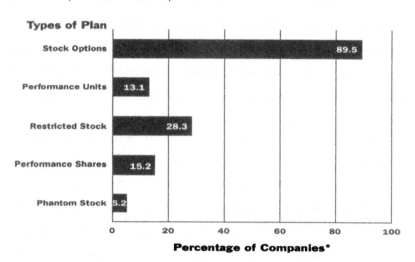

* Public companies only.

Source: Watson Wyatt Data Services.

Under an MSPP, employees purchase company restricted stock or restricted stock units (RSUs) on a pre-tax basis out of income that would otherwise be paid as salary or bonus.[2] Purchases are usually at a discount. For the employee, the discount helps balance the risk of foregoing current compensation to purchase stock with restrictions. Discounts typically range from 15 to 25 percent; a 20 percent discount appears reasonably appealing to employees and outside shareholders. However, the following factors may influence the discount amount: the performance of the stock and the industry, the length of the restriction period, the competitive environment and the need to foster employee stock ownership. Some companies use a "premium" or "matching" plan with the same economic result. For example, the executive receives one "free" share for every four he or she purchases.

In addition to encouraging stock ownership, the MSPP also achieves the following desirable objectives:

■ Adds another equity-based component to the company's executive compensation portfolio. (The MSPP can be particularly useful if options are under water and may be preferable to outright grants of restricted stock, since it is not "free" to the executive.)

■ Increases the portion of total direct compensation that is based on creating shareholder value.

■ Improves retention of managers by increasing the portion of compensation that they "leave on the table" if their employment is voluntarily terminated.

---

2 Restricted stock is actual stock of the company subject to designated restrictions. Restricted stock units are a notional account established for a participant that is credited with amounts equivalent to shares of company stock, subject to designated restrictions. At the time of payout, a participant receives a number of actual shares of company stock equal to the number of his or her RSUs.

- Reduces the cash flow of compensation expense.

- Provides incentives for both mandatory and voluntary or forced savings among management.

- Has favorable tax and accounting treatment.

- Can complement a qualified employee stock purchase plan with a 15 percent discount (IRC Section 423 plan).

- Can even allow for the conversion of supplemental retirement plans into stock.

Figure 6-4 summarizes the design of a typical plan.

Some very well-known companies use this type of program. MCI, the giant telecommunications company, pays part of its annual incentive in RSUs and allows for the remainder of the bonus to be used to buy additional shares at a 20 percent discount (equivalent to a 25 percent premium on a 1:4 match). Other companies that

Figure 6-4: Summary of an MSPP (example)

Plan Feature	Description of a Typical Plan
Participation	Eligibility is limited to designated members of senior management.
Form	Restricted Stock Units
Mandatory Purchases	Participants are required to use 25 percent of their bonus to make purchases.
Voluntary Purchases	Participants are allowed to make voluntary purchases not to exceed 50 percent of their bonus when combined with their mandatory purchases. Voluntary purchases for a bonus year must be elected by June 30 of that year.
Proxy Disclosure	Ownership of RSUs under the MSPP is included in stock ownership for proxy disclosure. However, an explanation of the RSUs needs to be footnoted.
Discount	Twenty percent discount — i.e., one matching unit for every four units purchased.
Restrictions/Vesting	Three years; additional deferral allowed.

use the MSPP are Officemax, The Sports Authority, Beazer Homes and Kmart, among dozens of others. The discounts range from 15 percent to 50 percent or more, with a median of 20 percent.

ANOTHER PROGRAM

Another program that can be very helpful in linking executive and shareholder interests is a Performance Share Plan (PSP — see Appendix A for a definition). This plan, which contingently grants shares of stock if certain performance goals are attained, can also be very effective in creating direct stock ownership without being a "giveaway." As part of a total compensation package, it can be a powerful signal to both executives and shareholders.

The choice of the performance goal is extremely important. Basically any financial or stock market measure, or a combination, can be utilized. A Total Return to Shareholders (TRS) is one of the best measures. The TRS measure can either be:

- in absolute value, such as 15 percent compounded over 3 years; or

- in relative terms, e.g., to beat the median TRS of the S&P 500.

If, for example, the company "beat the median," all of the shares would pay out.

"PREMIUM-PRICED" STOCK OPTIONS

Another stock incentive plan that has enjoyed popularity over the past few years is a "premium-priced" stock option, which has an exercise price above the market stock price on the date of the grant. For example, if the stock price is currently $20, a traditional stock option would have an exercise (or "strike") price of $20. A premium-priced option might have an exercise price of $30. During 1996,

Michael Eisner of Disney received a huge grant of stock options with premium prices.

This design delivers the message to executives and all employees that there is some minimum level of return to shareholders that is expected. In this case, a 4.1 percent compounded return over 10 years is the threshold level that must be achieved before the options have any value. The 4.1 percent is barely above the historical inflation level and below the return from a riskless government bond. If there is no minimum level of performance, there is no payout.

Numerous critics of executive pay, including some institutional investors, support premium options as a "no-brainer" solution to the executive pay dilemma. If the CEO and the executive team, working with all employees, beat the premium stock price, they will really deserve their pay.

Premium options are an excellent program, and they belong in the tool kit for executive pay experts and the companies they advise. But they are not a panacea, and if used improperly, could actually create additional problems.

The basic problem is that in order to achieve the premium stock price, in theory the management team would have to undertake a *riskier business strategy* than the market is currently anticipating for the company.[3] Naturally, if that strategy is successful, all the shareholders plus the option holders will benefit. If the stratgegy is not successful, the stock price will go down further than currently anticipated and the real shareholders will lose more than the option holders.

---

3 See *Value at the Top* for further explanation.

The premise of premium options is that the threshold or average return to stockholders (in this case, the 4.1 percent) is easily attainable. It also belies our core argument that the reason the average company in the United States is doing well is due to luck or random circumstances, and not at least partly due to the executive pay programs themselves. Nevertheless, when used in conjunction with other programs, specifically real stock programs, premium options have their place. Disney is a good example of a company facing only a small risk from their premium options, since CEO Eisner is such a large shareholder.

Consistent with the trend in executive pay to create more linkage with stock price, so has director pay itself moved in that direction. Most large publicly traded companies provide stock options or another stock plan for directors. This is strongly supported by institutional investors.

CONCLUSION

It is important to note that rising levels of executive stock ownership do pose risks to the executives themselves. Naturally, their personal portfolios are less diversified than they would otherwise be. During most of the 1990s, the U.S. stock market has done extraordinarily well — but who knows what the future holds. However, even if there is a market correction, high levels of executive stock ownership would still be the best long-term policy for the board, the shareholders, all employees and the executives themselves.

Rising levels of executive and all-employee stock ownership have a positive impact on company performance. Virtually every compensation program should be evaluated with regard to whether it creates additional stock ownership. It is well worth the effort.

Epilogue:
What if the
Bulls Stop
Running?

A s I write this in early spring 1997, the U.S. stock market has
been swooning over uncertainty about interest rates in the wake
of a rate rise by the Federal Reserve Board and despite continuing
high levels of profitability. This may be the start of a major
1970s-style bear market. We doubt it, however. Nevertheless,
even if the Dow Jones Industrial Average corrects by 25 percent
(to the low 5,000s), U.S. companies and the U.S. economy are
extremely well positioned to face the global pressures of the
third millennium. U.S. compensation programs — including
and especially those at the executive level — are flexible and
motivating enough to help weather this volatility.

Has the United States solved all of its economic problems? Do
Japan and Europe face less optimistic economic futures? Of course
not. However, we started by saying that using stock price as the
primary executive performance measure was a defining reform of

20th-century U.S. capitalism. While this has created some social issues, all stakeholders — employees, pension holders, customers, vendors and shareholders — have benefited in the aggregate from this change. Stock-based reward programs are one reason why the United States is winning the global economic war.

SELECTED BIBLIOGRAPHY

Becker, Gary. *Human Capital: A Theoretical and Empirical Analysis, with Special Reference to Education.* National Bureau of Economic Research, 1964.

Blair, Margaret M. *Ownership and Control: Rethinking Corporate Governance for the Twenty-First Century.* The Brookings Institution, 1995.

_____. Wealth Creation and Wealth Sharing: A Colloquium on Corporate Governance and Investments in Human Capital. The Brookings Institution, 1996.

_____. "CEO Pay: Why Such a Contentious Issue?" *The Brookings Review* (Winter 1994): 23–27.

Blinder, Alan S., ed. *Paying for Productivity: A Look at the Evidence.* The Brookings Institution, 1990.

Bok, Derek. *The Cost of Talent: How Executives and Professionals Are Paid and How It Affects America.* The Free Press, 1993.

Council of Institutional Investors. *Does Ownership Add Value? A Collection of 100 Empirical Studies.* September 1994.

Crystal, Graef S. *The Crystal Report.* 1995, 1996.

Crystal, Graef S. and Frederic W. Cook. "The Growing Pay Gap: Are CEOs Paid Too Much Relative to Other Employees?" *ACA Journal* (Summer 1996): 22–29.

Davis, Steven J., John C. Haltiwanger and Scott Schuh. *Job Creation and Destruction.* MIT Press, 1996.

Deavers, Ken. "Soaring Profits, Stagnating Real Wages: Not the Real Story." *ACA News* (March 1996): 12–14.

Financial Accounting Standards Board. "Accounting for Stock-based Compensation." Financial Accounting Standards Board, 1995.

Frank, Robert H. and Philip J. Cook. *The Winner-Take-All Society.* The Free Press, 1995.

Fukuyama, Francis. *Trust: The Social Virtues & The Creation of Prosperity.* The Free Press, 1995.

Kaplan, Steven N. "Top Executive Rewards and Firm Performance: A Comparison of Japan and the United States." *Journal of Political Economy* (1994): 510–546.

Kay, Ira T. *Value at the Top: Solutions to the Executive Compensation Crisis.* HarperBusiness, 1992.

Kay, Ira T., Howard J. Peyser and Kjeld Sorensen. "Using Restricted Stock or Restricted Stock Units to Increase Management Ownership." *Journal of Deferred Compensation: Non-qualified Plans and Executive Compensation* (Spring 1996): 27–43.

Kay, Ira T. and Rodney F. Robinson. "Misguided Attacks on Executive Pay Hurt Shareholders." *Compensation and Benefits Review* (January–February 1994): 25–33.

Langsam, Sheldon, Jerry Kreuze and Gale Newell. "Comparison Between Pension Benefit Guaranty Corporation and Financial Statement Disclosures of Pension Plan Underfunding." *The Journal of Accounting and Finance* (Autumn 1996): 105–117.

McAdams, Jerry. *The Reward Plan Advantage.* Jossey-Bass Publishers, 1996.

National Association of Corporate Directors. *Report of the NACD Blue Ribbon Commission on Executive Compensation: Guidelines for Corporate Directors.* NACD, 1993.

Ozaki, Robert. *Human Capitalism: The Japanese Enterprise System as World Model.* Kodansha International, Ltd., 1991.

Roach, Stephen S. "The Hollow Ring of the Productivity Revival," *Harvard Business Review* (November–December 1996): 81–89.

Seltzer, Irwin M. "Are CEOs Overpaid?" *The Public Interest* (Winter 1997): 26–38.

Tezuka, Hiroyuki. "Success as the Source of Failure? Competition and Cooperation in the Japanese Economy." *Sloan Management Review* (Winter 1997): 83–93.

Thurow, Lester C. *Head to Head: The Coming Economic Battle Among Japan, Europe and America.* William Morrow & Company, Inc., 1992.

Waterman, Robert H., Jr. *What America Does Right: Learning from Companies That Put People First.* W.W. Norton & Company, 1994.

Watson Wyatt Worldwide. *Directors Survey.* Watson Wyatt Worldwide, 1996.

Wyatt-Seikei. *Top Management Compensation.* Japan, 1994.

Yamamoto, Masao. "Japanese Companies Need Stock Options to Compete." *Tokyo Business* (January 1996): 24–26.

APPENDIX A

Types of Long-Term Incentive Plans

A long-term incentive plan is an arrangement designed to reward an individual for corporate performance over a period of more than a year. Even though the corporation may make grants and ultimately payouts every year, what defines these plans is the longer-term performance period. Generally, the compensation value of these plans depends upon the corporation's future performance and events, as opposed to an annual incentive plan, which is based on the company's past performance and events. Thus, even though an annual incentive plan may provide for payments to be deferred in equivalent-value stock units or in restricted stock, it is not a long-term incentive plan because the corporation bases the award's compensation value on performance during the past year, rather than on performance over a future period of years.

The following is a description of the most common types of long-term incentive plans in the United States.

STOCK OPTIONS

Stock option plans offer an executive the right to purchase a specified number of shares of the corporation's stock at a specified price during a specified period of time.

1. In an **incentive stock option** (ISO), or qualified stock option plan, for example, the corporation gives the executive (or other employee) the right to purchase, say, 1,000 shares of the company's stock at $50 per share at any time during the next 10 years. Typically, the exercise price, $50, is the same as the stock's actual price on the date of the grant. It does not have to be that way, but it usually is.

   Three years later, if the stock is trading at $80 per share, the employee could write a check for $50,000 and receive 1,000 shares of stock, now worth $80,000. The employee's $30,000 paper profit incurs no tax liability until he or she sells the stock.

2. A **non-qualified stock option** (NQSO), sometimes referred to as a "non-statutory stock option," does not meet all the requirements for incentive stock options. Nevertheless, non-qualified options usually have a 10-year option term and are usually priced at 100 percent of market value at time of grant.

   In a non-qualified plan, the employee pays ordinary income

tax rates at the time he or she exercises the option. Using the previous example, the employee would pay tax on the $30,000 paper profit as though it were ordinary income. Typically, employees have to sell some shares to pay the taxes. The company does get a $30,000 tax deduction, so a non-qualified stock option plan is advantageous to the company.

Since today's tax rates are basically the same for capital gains and ordinary income, most companies issue non-qualified plans so they can obtain the tax deduction, which helps their cash flow. If ordinary income tax rates increase or capital gains rates drop, the situation can change. Because of such tax rate changes, incentive stock options have gained and lost popularity two or three times in corporate history.

STOCK AND UNIT PLANS

3. A **performance share plan** (PSP) contingently grants stock to an executive. These performance share grants entitle the executive to stock shares at time of payment if the company achieves predetermined financial objectives. The value of the stock may appreciate or decline between the initial award and the payment date. The number of shares that become payable, if any, depends on the extent to which the objectives are achieved.

In such a plan, the company tells the employee, in effect, "You have 1,000 performance shares. Two things influence how much you ultimately receive: the company's financial performance, which will influence the number of shares, and the stock price, which will determine the value of the shares." Total Return to Shareholders (TRS) also is becoming a common measure in these plans.

4. A **performance unit plan** (PUP) contingently grants units that entitle an executive to cash payments (or their equivalent in stock) valued at the time of award if the company achieves predetermined objectives. The unit value remains constant. A performance unit plan is similar in most respects to a performance share plan, except that the value the executive receives relates to the value placed upon a share or unit at the time of grant. The value of the original units does not appreciate or decline.

For example, assume the employee has a goal of achieving a return on equity of 20 percent per year over the next three years. If the company achieves that target, the employee receives a performance unit payment of, say, $50,000. If the return on equity is above the goal, the company pays a bonus greater than $50,000; if lower than 20 percent, the bonus is smaller. Frequently, if return on equity falls below a certain threshold level, say 12 percent, there is no payment. If it goes above a certain level, say 30 percent, frequently the payouts are capped. But these are all design features, subject to board and management discussion in designing the program.

5. In **restricted stock plans**, the company makes awards in the form of actual shares of company stock, not the appreciation or the profit on the stock. The company transfers actual shares of stock to the employee, but they carry certain restrictions, such as prohibitions against disposition or

rights of first refusal, and they may be subject to substantial risk of forfeiture. The restrictions mean that the employee cannot sell the stock until it vests or until the restrictions lapse.

Companies also have been granting what is called performance-accelerated restricted stock (PARS). If restrictions typically would lapse in three, four or five years, the plan allows restrictions to lapse sooner if the company attains certain higher levels of financial performance.

In addition, many companies use restricted stock as part of their stock purchase plans, as discussed in Chapter 6.

6. A **phantom stock option** grants a number of units to an executive, each of which creates rights to a payment equal to any appreciation that occurs in the market value of company stock between the date of grant and some future date, often accompanied by dividend equivalent payments. It is almost exclusively used for private companies or subsidiaries that do not have market-valued stock and do not want minority shareholders. It differs from other stock incentive plans in that the company transfers no stock to a participating executive. Although companies usually use stock units to determine the payment amount an executive may receive, the company transfers no equity interest to the executive, issues no stock certificates and pays no dividends. The executive receives a simulation of stock ownership. Since a phantom stock option plan is an appreciation plan, the executive never receives the initial value of the units or shares granted, but rather receives the

future appreciation or income (dividend equivalents) attributable to those units. The value of the phantom stock is determined either by a professional appraisal or by some type of economic or financial formula.

The "Value" of an Employee Stock Option: A Brief Discussion of the Black-Scholes Option Pricing Model

An option to buy stock is a valuable right, whether for outside investors or an executive. Outside purchasers of options (for example, on the Chicago Board of Options Exchange) have a market to determine current value. They also use sophisticated mathematical models, such as Black-Scholes, among many others, to estimate an option's value. These models can be useful in valuing an executive option as well.

A Black-Scholes calculation yields an executive option value that ranges from five to 80 percent of the market price for an "at the money" option (strike price = market price). The variables that influence an option's value include: dividends, price volatility, etc. (See Table B-1 for further explanation.) For a "typical" stock with "typical" price volatility, a four percent dividend and 10 years until expiration, the option value would be *around* 30 percent. This means that if the current stock price is $30, and the option's strike price is also $30, then the option itself is worth around $9 (30 percent of $30). It is important to remember that when an outside investor exercises the option, he or she must pay, in this example, the full $30 for the shares. The price the investor paid for the option ($9) is not credited toward the purchase price. Therefore, the option's break-even price is $39, which reflects the option's very high value.

Because the executive option holder usually does not pay for the option itself, he or she receives a very valuable right for "free."

Since executives do not pay for their options, they have great difficulty valuing them. As a result, our experience shows that they tend to undervalue them. It is true that without an external market, options are difficult to value. Valuation depends on the stock price, the strike price, the stock's dividend rate, the risk-free interest rate available on the open market, the time until expiration and the stock's volatility, among other factors. Most option pricing models, including Black-Scholes, incorporate these factors. The following table shows the impact of each.

In general, the Black-Scholes model depicts a present value of a future profit on a stock option. Using historical data, it calculates the various probabilities that the stock will hit various prices. It

Table B-1: Factors that Influence an Option's Value

Factor	Impact on Option's Value	Comments
Stock Price	Positive*	A 10 percent increase in a high-price stock means a larger dollar value than a 10 percent increase in a low-price stock.
Strike (Exercise) Price	Negative**	The higher the strike price, the greater the stock price must increase for the option to have value.
Dividend Rate	Negative	A higher dividend means the company has less cash to invest to create stock price increases.
Risk-Free Interest Rate	Positive	If the buyer borrows money to buy the stock (instead of the option), a higher interest rate increases the cost of borrowing. This makes the option more valuable.
Time until Expiration	Positive	The longer the time, the greater the likelihood the stock price will increase.
Volatility	Positive	The more volatile the price, the more likely the stock price will rise above the option price.

* "Positive" means that an increase in the factor yields an increase in the value (price) of the option.

**"Negative" means that an increase in the factor yields a decrease in the value (price) of the option.

Source: Kay, Ira T. *Value at the Top: Solutions to the Executive Compensation Crisis.*

then multiplies those probabilities and prices and takes the present value. It is usually expressed in dollars and as a percent of today's stock price. It is used for a number of purposes:

- Valuing options as part of an analysis of the total worth of an employee's compensation program;

- A *pro-forma* or an actual accounting expense under current U.S. accounting rules; and

- An estimated value of top executive grants for disclosure purposes in proxy statements. (This is required under current U.S. securities law. As an alternative, companies are allowed to show a future value of the options by assuming 5 or 10 percent stock price growth rates. This future value is not comparable to the present value generated by the Black-Scholes formula.)

Printed in the United States
by Baker & Taylor Publisher Services